DATE DUE

c.1

921
LaF

Brown, Marion
    Susette La
Flesche, advocate
for Native American
rights.

Susette La Flesche

Advocate for Native American Rights

by Marion Marsh Brown

Consultant: Jay Miller, Ph.D.
D'Arcy McNickle Center for the History of the American Indian
The Newberry Library
Chicago, Illinois

 CHILDRENS PRESS®
CHICAGO

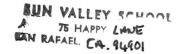

PICTURE ACKNOWLEDGMENTS

Omaha World-Herald — Frontispiece, 18 (2 photos), 38, 44

Nebraska State Historical Society — 8, 26, 32, 58 (2 photos), 59 (2 photos), 60 (4 photos), 61 (3 photos), 62 (3 photos), 63 (2 photos), 64 (2 photos), 82, 86, 90, 98, 102

Historical Society of Douglas County/Library Archives/Center, Omaha, Nebraska — 12

Cover illustration by Len W. Meents

Library of Congress Cataloging-in-Publication Data

Brown, Marion Marsh.
    Susette La Flesche: (advocate for native american rights)/by Marion Marsh Brown.
    p. cm. — (People of distinction)
    Includes index.
    Summary: Describes the life of the Omaha Indian woman who fought for Indians' rights, becoming the first American Indian lecturer and the first published Indian artist.
    ISBN 0-516-03277-1
    1. La Flesche, Susette, 1854-1903 — Juvenile literature. 2. Omaha Indians — Biography — Juvenile literature. 3. Omaha Indians — Civil rights — Juvenile literature. 4. Omaha Indians — Social conditions — Juvenile literature. [1. La Flesche, Susette, 1854-1903. 2. Civil rights workers. 3. Omaha Indians — Biography. 4. Indians of North America — Biography.] I. Title. II. Series.
    E99.04L343   1992
    973'.04975 — dc20
    [B]   91-35296
                                                                         CIP
                                                                          AC

Table of Contents

Chapter 1
Friends in Trouble   9

Chapter 2
A Father's Promise   13

Chapter 3
Enter Thomas Tibbles   15

Chapter 4
Victorious Verdict   19

Chapter 5
Alarming Proposal   21

Chapter 6
Tears and Triumph   27

Chapter 7
"Bright Eyes"   33

Chapter 8
Tragic News   39

Chapter 9
Authors Ahoy!   45

Chapter 10
"Law is Liberty"   49

Chapter 11
"Nedawi"   53

Chapter 12
A Measure of Success   65

Chapter 13
  Wedding Vows   67

Chapter 14
  Visit to Standing Bear   71

Chapter 15
  East Again   75

Chapter 16
  Double Success   79

Chapter 17
  Living Like Whites   83

Chapter 18
  New Challenge   87

Chapter 19
  A Year Abroad   91

Chapter 20
  Return to the Capital   95

Chapter 21
  Oo-Mah-Ha Ta-Wa-Tha   99

Chapter 22
  Home on the Reservation   103

Time Line   106

Index   111

About the Author   117

Joseph "Iron Eye" La Flesche, the distinguished chief of the Omahas

Chapter 1

FRIENDS IN TROUBLE

There were four of them, the La Flesche sisters, daughters of Iron Eye, Joseph La Flesche, the famous head chief of the Omaha Indians. They lived on a reservation in the Midwest state of Nebraska. The reservation was comprised of thousands of acres of grassy, tree-splotched, rolling hills that looked down on the fast-flowing Missouri River below. Here and there the vast expanse of grasslands was broken by a huddled group of dwellings in the midst of cultivated fields.

The settlement in which the La Flesche family lived differed vastly in appearance from the others. It was made up of frame houses, some of them two stories in height, whereas the other settlements were comprised of rounded earth lodges with domed roofs. Joseph La Flesche built the first house in what was called "The Make-Believe White-Man Village," as a start of what he foresaw as a necessary change from the Indians' tribal ways of life to the white people's ways of living. "There are so many of them," he had said, referring to whites. "They come like bees swarming."

The year was 1876, and it was a year of turmoil—the first of many, for the Omaha tribe. Just now they had received bad news. The Ponca tribe, in which they had many relatives, was to be moved from its reservation in Dakota Territory to what was known as the Indian Territory in Oklahoma.

Susette, twenty-two years old and the eldest of the La Flesche sisters, was preparing to ride horseback with her father on a long journey. They were going to meet the Poncas at the point where they would cross the Platte River on their long march south. They wanted to visit briefly with their relatives and to tell them good-bye, for they doubted that they would ever see them again. White Swan, a chief of the Poncas, was Iron Eye's half-brother. Susette was looking forward to seeing her uncle and aunt and cousins as they paused on their long trek to the unwelcome territory.

The younger La Flesche girls who ranged from fifteen to eleven years old—Rosalie, Marguerite, and Susan—were helping with the travelers' preparations. Their chatter was quiet, though they were excited and disturbed. Iron Eye stomped in and out, his wooden leg clumping with each step, his face a thundercloud and Frank, the son of the family, fetched and carried provisions. Susette, although very concerned about what was happening to the Poncas, spoke little.

Mary, the mother of the family, and Nicomi, the grand-mother, scurried about in the kitchen handing jerky and fresh-baked bread to the girls to be packed in the travelers' saddlebags.

Not only was the scurrying little family upset about what was happening to their relatives—being forced to leave their homeland—there also was fear in their hearts for their own future. If the government could remove the Poncas from their reservation, might not the same thing happen to the Omahas?

When, after a week's absence, Susette and her father returned home, they were met with a barrage of questions: How was Uncle White Swan? The children? Were they actually on their way south? The answers came slowly, sadly. Yes, they were on their way, depressed and fearful—fearful of the five-hundred-mile trek that lay before them and of what they would find at its end.

Susette and Iron Eye had watched with heavy hearts as the Poncas crossed the wide waters of the Platte and disappeared into the distance, driven like cattle by soldiers in blue.

Standing Bear and his family, left to right: Walk-in-the-wind,
an orphaned grandson; Standing Bear; Sunshine, Standing Bear's
only living child; Susette, Standing Bear's wife; and Light
of the way, an orphaned niece

Chapter 2

A FATHER'S PROMISE

One day the following spring, excitement again ran high on the Omaha Reservation, and the La Flesche sisters were in the midst of it. On a raw, windy day in March a small straggling band of ragged, half-starved, foot-weary Poncas appeared at Iron Eye's door seeking refuge. The girls' excitement gave way to anger as, little by little, while the decrepit, dispirited group was being warmed and fed, their story came out.

Standing Bear, their leader, was the spokesperson. The Poncas' first year in the Indian Territory had been disastrous, he began. The land was so poor that they had been unable to raise decent crops, and so they did not have enough to eat. Unused to the hot, dry climate, and with inadequate food, many became ill. At least a third of the tribe had died from sickness.

The Indian death wail rose from the listeners, but Standing Bear raised his hand for silence. He had more to tell. Among those who had died was his eldest son. Now the wild wailing broke out again, young voices lifting with the old.

When Standing Bear had quieted them, he recounted the sad climax of his story. When he lay dying, he said, his son had begged to have his body returned for burial in the land where he had grown up and which he loved, their homeland. His father had promised that this would be done.

So with a few loyal friends, Standing Bear had slipped away from the territory, with his son's bones in a wooden box on a rickety wagon pulled by two old nags. Among them the little band had only twenty dollars and a small supply of food. Before them lay five hundred miles.

Avoiding white settlements for fear of being reported and taken back to the territory, they had trudged doggedly on. Winter overtook them, adding to their trials. But at long last, here they were with friends, where they hoped to linger long enough to gain the strength to go the remaining hundred or so miles to the land that had once been theirs.

Iron Eye's daughters were happy when their father offered a temporary home on the Omaha reservation to the handful of weary, footsore Poncas. Things looked even brighter for them when Iron Eye told them they would be welcome to a plot of land where they could plant and raise a crop. The girls were proud of their father for making this thoughtful offer. It seemed a sensible way to help their destitute friends.

But they were not to see the plan put into action. Instead, they soon were to watch with horror a dramatic new scene in their visitors' sad story. This time Susette would be involved. It was only the beginning of her long involvement with the Poncas' problems.

Chapter 3

ENTER THOMAS TIBBLES

The Poncas were barely rested from their long journey when one morning there was a loud pounding on Iron Eye's door. A bevy of soldiers, who said they were from Fort Crook, a fort just north of the city of Omaha, had arrived. They demanded to know where the Poncas were. They had come to arrest them for leaving the territory.

So the La Flesche sisters, who had witnessed the woeful arrival of the Ponca band, now witnessed their forced removal. They were rounded up to be marched to Fort Omaha where they would be imprisoned. But what could be done about it?

Iron Eye's decision was immediate. He would go to Omaha City. Susette must come with him as his interpreter. There was a newspaper reporter he had heard about who had written some articles at the time the Poncas were removed to the territory, protesting the action. Perhaps he could help.

Whenever the need arose for Iron Eye to converse with whites, he depended on Susette to interpret for him. Being the eldest, she had already received a good education. After the mission school, where the barest basics of elementary education were taught, and which of itself furnished more education than most of the girls of the tribe received, Susette had been sent to a girls' boarding school in Elizabeth, New Jersey. She had learned to speak the English language fluently.

Susette's sisters accepted her responsible position in the family, for they respected their father's judgment. They knew he was both wise and fair. He had recently made arrangements for two more of the girls to enter Elizabeth Institute in the fall. This opportunity had been offered first to Rosalie and Susan, but Rosalie had asked to remain on the reservation. Ed Farley, a young man from an Irish immigrant family who worked on the reservation, had asked Rosalie to marry him. She had accepted his proposal joyfully. So the privilege of an Eastern education fell to Susan and Marguerite.

When Susette and her father arrived in Omaha City, they soon learned that Mr. Tibbles, the reporter they were seeking, knew of the imprisonment of Standing Bear and the Poncas with him. He had already written articles that had appeared in *The World Herald*, the paper where he was assistant editor, protesting the government's heartless action. Through these articles, considerable sympathy had been aroused for the ill-treated Indians.

Mr. Tibbles, they were told, had gone to Fort Omaha to report the meeting between Standing Bear and the commander of the fort, General Crook. In his story Mr. Tibbles had even quoted some of the exact words spoken between the two. The general, after hearing Standing Bear's story, had said he was sorry, but his orders were to return the Poncas to the Indian Territory. He could not disobey orders from Washington. All of this Mr. Tibbles had brought to the public through his articles.

The general's decision meant that the Poncas might be escorted on their way to the Indian Territory at any moment. Mr. Tibbles had consulted with a highly respected attorney, John L. Webster. Wasn't there something that could be done, Mr. Tibbles had asked? A writ of habeas corpus, perhaps?

Mr. Webster had agreed that the purpose of such a writ was to bring to court the proposition that a person was being "wrongfully detained," illegally imprisoned. In the present situation, however, he saw a problem because the person involved was an Indian, and Indians, like children, were considered wards of the state. Mr. Webster had said he would like a little time to think about the matter. Perhaps he would talk it over with attorney J.M. Poppleton.

Susette had translated all of this information from Mr. Tibbles for her father, rapidly, from English to Omaha.

Mr. Tibbles ended by saying that time was being wasted. They had to get some results.

This was Susette's first encounter with Thomas Henry Tibbles, but it would be far from her last.

John L. Webster (top) and J.M. Poppleton (bottom) were the lawyers who worked on the writ of habeus corpus to submit to the court to show that Standing Bear and the Poncas with him were being wrongfully detained.

Chapter 4

VICTORIOUS VERDICT

The two lawyers, Webster and Poppleton, were working on the writ of habeas corpus to submit to the court. The biggest problem was time. The Poncas were likely to be taken south to the Indian Territory at any moment. Iron Eye decided he and Susette should remain in the city. They could at least give the Poncas moral support. Susette was pleased with her father's decision. It would be very hard to wait back on the reservation for word of what was happening to their friends. Besides, Mr. Tibbles had asked her to help in keeping a running account of the situation in *The World Herald*. He himself was busy with his job on the paper, and he was also writing and sending off stories to other papers about the plight of Standing Bear. He assured Susette that anyone who spoke as well as she did could certainly write. She knew the facts, and he was sure she could present them clearly and forcibly.

So while they waited for the lawyers to draw up the writ of habeas corpus and for the judge who was to hear it to arrive in town, Susette wrote her first newspaper copy.

When Mr. Tibbles showed her a copy of the petition on which so much rested, it gave her hope. In part it read, "Your complainants were not violating and are not guilty of any violation of any law of the United States...or of any treaty of the United States, for which said arrest and imprisonment were made." Surely anyone could see that the Indians should be freed, thought Susette, that there was no just reason and no legal right for the Poncas' imprisonment.

The courtroom was packed on April 30, the date finally set for the hearing. When the case was continued for a second day, the crowd returned, including Susette and her father. Judge Dundy took several days to consider the testimony and arguments. When his decision was handed down, Susette didn't even need to interpret for her father. The happy faces, the loud applause, and backslapping told the story.

When the words "An Indian is a person within the meaning of the law" were read, jubilant shouts rang out. Then the crowd quieted to hear the rest of the words, "...and has the right to sue out a writ of habeas corpus in a federal court."

They had won!

While all who had worked on the case realized this was not the end, that there would be suits and countersuits to follow, they also knew that a giant step forward had been taken for American Indians with those five words of Judge Dundy's:

"An Indian is a person..."

To Susette no words would ever be more beautiful.

Chapter 5

ALARMING PROPOSAL

Susette and her father returned to the reservation in high spirits. However, Susette explained to the family, this was only the beginning. The two good men, the lawyers who had handled the writ of habeas corpus that released Standing Bear and his companions from jail, had said so. They believed that many trials lay ahead before Indians' rights would be properly recognized.

The time was drawing near for Marguerite and Susan to leave for Elizabeth Institute, and Susette, having been there before them, took the responsibility of preparing them. They had never been away from home. They had never ridden on a train. They had never seen a city. And they had certainly never lived among white people—the hardest thing of all for them to imagine.

When the day of departure arrived, Susette and Iron Eye took the girls to the train depot. Their trunks rode with them in Iron Eye's spring wagon, pulled by two dapper Indian ponies. When they arrived at the station, Susette bought their tickets and saw them on the belching black train, making sure that they had the bundle containing the food for their meals en route. Susette felt sure that Susan, the more aggressive of the two, would take care of Marguerite who, although the older, was more delicate and often ill.

Not long after Susette had seen her two sisters off for the East, the newspaper reporter, Mr. Tibbles, came to the reservation and asked Susette to interpret for him as he laid a proposition before Iron Eye. As she translated his fast-paced words, she could see merit in the plan. Money, he said, was needed to continue the fight for Indian rights, and he had conceived a speaking tour as the answer. Not only would it bring in money, it also would alert the general public to the plight of the Indians. Public sympathy would bring pressure on Congress and on the secretary of the interior in whose department the Bureau of Indian Affairs operated.

Tibbles' voice rose in excitement as he came to the climax of his plan: A speaking tour featuring Standing Bear and Susette would take the country by storm!

Susette blanched. She could not believe what she was hearing. What an impossible, terrifying idea!

Tibbles quit speaking, looking to Iron Eye for his reaction. Susette's eyes too turned to her father, and when she saw the fierce expression on his face and he began to speak, she knew relief. Of course, he said, Susette could take no part in such a plan. He would not think of letting his daughter go off with two men on any kind of tour. Otherwise, Tibbles' plan sounded good.

Mr. Tibbles, however, fired with his idea, had a ready suggestion to meet Iron Eye's objection. Couldn't Susette's brother Frank, almost a man, accompany them as a sort of chaperon for Susette?

This gave Iron Eye pause and, always eager to help his people, he finally agreed that this might be possible. He would give Mr. Tibbles an answer after he had thought about this and talked it over with his wife Mary.

Susette was overwhelmed with fear. She had always been afraid of having to meet new situations. From the time that she experienced "The Turning of the Child," the ceremony in which at age four she had received her tribal name, *Ishtatheanba* (Bright Eyes), up to the present moment—at the age of twenty-three—she had been fearful of new and different situations.

She did not remember much about the ceremony, just that she had been placed on a big rock inside the ceremonial tent and turned in each of the four directions by a chanting warrior who had seemed very big to her. And she did remember her pleasure at the end of the ceremony when her feet were thrust into new moccasins. But the vivid memory, which had never left her, was of the terror she felt when her mother had opened the tent flap and pushed her gently into the ceremonial tent to face alone whatever lay within.

Later, when she was eight and Iron Eye, ever mindful of the importance of education if his people were to survive in the white people's world, enrolled her in the mission school, she had been very apprehensive. And of course when she had been sent east to Elizabeth Institute, she had been terribly frightened.

After that, the next time she remembered having the old sensations of a pounding heart, shaking knees, and the inability to find her voice was when she opened her own school. On the first morning, she had stood before her roomful of assorted pupils, opened her mouth to greet them, and no sound came. She had worked so hard to get the school. It had taken two years after her graduation from Elizabeth Institute to get permission from Washington to start a school, even though the mission school had been closed and there was no educational facility on the reservation. Then it had taken time to find a usable building, get it repaired and meagerly furnished, and to obtain a few books and supplies. She had been so determined to open the school, so eager, and yet she had been so nervous on the first day of school that her voice had deserted her.

Remembering this last situation, she felt sure she could never speak from a platform to a white audience, as Tibbles was asking her to do. So it was with a shock of disbelief when later she heard her father's decision that, with Frank along as chaperon, she could go.

Iron Eye's decisions were law. She knew that there was no escape from the terrifying ordeal that lay ahead for her. The only consolation she could find lay in the fact that, in each of the past situations which she had faced with such dread, the end result had been good. Each, once her fear was conquered, had brought her success and satisfaction.

Susette's mother, Mary Gale La Flesche

Chapter 6

TEARS AND TRIUMPH

Susette's preparations for the Eastern trip were almost complete. Mary and Nicomi had helped her getting a suitable wardrobe in shape. Susette had decided on dark dresses only, with just white collars and some colorful scarves to brighten them. Mary, though a woman of high intelligence, followed the traditional pattern of an Indian mother, usually remaining in the background. She was nevertheless essential in her role: drying skins, fashioning clothing, doing bead work, jerking meat (drying in thin strips), and cooking for the family. Mary was a quiet, gentle mother who loved each of her children with a deep devotion.

It was Tibbles' plan that they make Chicago the first city on their tour and work east from there. Still very worried about what lay ahead of her, yet wanting sincerely to help secure better conditions for her people, Susette felt torn and unsettled.

There was another disturbing aspect of her life also. Susette had been living among Indians as an Indian for some years now, ever since her return from Elizabeth Institute. Soon she would be living in the white world again as she had at boarding school, but this time as an adult. Not being sure of her identity was unsettling too.

Before the time of departure for the tour arrived, an even more shocking situation was to confront her. Again it was Mr. Tibbles who was the bearer of ill tidings. He said he had wonderful news. Bishop Clarkson of the Omaha Diocese had arranged for them to appear in a large church in Omaha before they left.

Susette put up a strong protest, but to no avail. T.H. Tibbles like Iron Eye, always had his way. The date was already set, he explained, and the event announced.

All too soon for Susette, the appointed day for the Omaha appearance arrived, and she set out for the city, accompanied by her old symptoms of fright. Tibbles had said that she was just to tell Standing Bear's story, which she knew well, and that her audience would be sympathetic. She told herself that it shouldn't be too bad, for it was true that she knew Standing Bear's story very well. She had been witness to much of it.

But when they arrived at the church and she saw the rows of filled seats, she lost any slight confidence she had built up. She sat with Tibbles and Standing Bear on the platform and looked down on the audience. How could she possibly go through with this? She felt positively ill.

It seemed only a minute until Tibbles was introducing Standing Bear, who stood up proudly in his best buckskins. The audience responded with an enthusiastic round of applause. Standing Bear sat down, and then it was Susette's turn.

Susette rose and moved forward to stand beside Tibbles at

the lectern. He introduced her as Bright Eyes, daughter of the Omaha chief Iron Eye, and said that she would relate Standing Bear's story. Then he returned to his chair.

Alone at the lectern, Susette found matters just as they had been on her first day of teaching. She tried to speak, but no sound came. She cleared her dry throat and tried again. This time a thin, frightened voice came weakly from her throat, but it strengthened as she proceeded. She began by telling her audience that Standing Bear was of the Ponca tribe, a tribe with very close ties to her own, the Omaha. She had many relatives among the Poncas, she said, including her father's half-brother and family. Then she told how the Poncas were forced to leave their beloved land on the Niobrara River in northern Nebraska and Dakota Territory and were taken to the Indian Territory. She described the impossibly bad conditions they found upon reaching the territory: the heat and dust, the lack of food and supplies, the illness and death.

The audience was attentive as she told the story, using excellent English, with vivid bits of description. Then she came to the part where Standing Bear and his little band had arrived at her father's house. Her voice began to choke as she tried to tell of their condition. She said they had *walked* five hundred miles, supplied with inadequate food and clothing. With her voice breaking, she said they looked more like skeletons than men.

Then she started to tell why they had come on this exhausting trip. She told in some detail about the sickness that had brought so many of the tribe to their beds after their arrival at the territory. This brought her to Standing Bear's own personal tragedy, the illness of his son. The tears came as she told of the youth's death and the final request he had made of his father—that he be buried not in the territory but back in the land from which they had come.

She tried to tell them then about Standing Bear's determination to carry out his son's request, to return his bones for burial in the earth of their homeland. It was too much. She burst into sobs. She could not go on. With her hands over her face, she stumbled back to her chair. She felt utterly disgraced. She had failed on her first attempt at public speaking. She had not even reached the climax of the story: Standing Bear's arrest, the writ of habeas corpus, Judge Dundy's wonderful words, "An Indian is a person," and Standing Bear's release from jail.

But the evening was not over. Tibbles pulled her to her feet to face the audience along with Standing Bear. She saw then that the people were standing and clapping furiously. She did not understand.

A woman on the greeting committee whom Susette had met earlier came up and took her by the arm and led her to the people, who were swarming to the front of the church. Women were crying and men were honking into their handkerchiefs. Susette was engulfed by people, patting her, hugging her, squeezing her hand. All were praising her, telling her how her story had touched them, how sorry they were about the mistreatment of the Indians. Susette could not believe what was happening. Even with her disgraceful conduct, she had not been considered a failure by her first audience.

Frank and Susette La Flesche

Chapter 7

"BRIGHT EYES"

Knowing some consolation from Mr. Tibbles' assurance that she had done well at her appearance in Omaha and more from the warmth with which the audience had received her, Susette tried hard to bury her fear of what lay ahead as she and her three male companions boarded the train for Chicago. Mr. Tibbles kept telling her that they needed to *dramatize* the plight of the Indians and that her breaking down at the Omaha meeting had fit perfectly into the picture. Nevertheless, she did not want to make such a spectacle of herself again. She would steel herself against emotion.

She asked Tibbles why he had introduced her as "Bright Eyes," and he said it hadn't just happened, that indeed he had planned it and he intended to introduce her by this name each time they appeared in public. When Susette asked "Why?" he answered that the Indian name fit her well and that its very sound had a romantic appeal. Just when she had thought she was to have the role of a white woman, she was to be introduced as an Indian! This continual seesaw, Indian to white and white to Indian, was not an easy adjustment.

While Tibbles dealt with the Indian Committee in setting up lecture dates and meetings with influential men who might offer financial help for the eastern tour, Susette and her brother visited places in Chicago that she thought would be interesting. She was most impressed with the library and the art museum, and reported to Tibbles that she found the city quite exciting. She liked the busy streets with their horse-drawn trams and carriages, and she especially enjoyed the way the gas lights bloomed at night, dispelling the darkness. During this time she could almost forget her reason for being there.

The sightseeing came to an end when Tibbles announced that they were set for their first public meeting. As the time for it drew near, Susette tried to think of her mission. If Mr. Tibbles could turn his life upside down, leaving his wife and two little girls and giving up his newspaper job to fight for improved conditions for the Indians, surely she, an Indian, could do her part.

The plan for their first appearance in Chicago differed from the one followed in Omaha. This time Standing Bear was to tell his own story with Susette interpreting. Then she was to give a talk. Tibbles had suggested that it would be well for her to write out her speech in advance, so this she had done. She had decided she would talk about just three of the major problems the Indians had with the United States government:

1. The government's breaking treaties that the Indians had signed in good faith.

2. The Indians' displacement from their lands. (She had two current examples of this: the Poncas

being moved to Indian Territory and a bill presently in Congress to do the same to her own tribe, the Omahas.)

3. The Indians' inability to make themselves heard in Washington.

Susette had her speech in her hand as she approached the lectern. She had told herself over and over that there was nothing to fear tonight. She could even read the speech if necessary. But reassuring herself had done no good. The same old symptoms of stage fright: squeamish stomach, sweaty palms, and shaking knees assailed her. She gritted her teeth. This time she was going to turn in a respectable performance, no matter what. And although she had a little trouble with her voice at first, it soon settled down and she was able to speak clearly. It helped that she could feel the audience was receptive.

The same pattern was followed in succeeding appearances in Chicago. Tibbles reported that sufficient monies had come in to sustain them throughout their stay there and to get them on to their next stop, Pittsburgh. There was just one aspect of this time in Chicago that did not please him. They were not getting coverage in the press. This was needed, he said, to influence a wider public and the wheels of government.

So Tibbles was delighted when one morning he received a call from a local newspaper asking for an interview with Bright Eyes. Susette, however, was not delighted. She did not anticipate the meeting with a reporter with any degree of pleasure. This would be another new experience and so it was frightening. But if it would help publicize the Indians' problems, Susette would make the best of it.

The reporter did not make things easy for her. She thought him positively antagonistic to her, and he exhibited no understanding of her race. Nonetheless, she held her ground, and when he asked her what she was trying to accomplish by making speeches in Chicago, she answered: "I am here to inform white people of the wrongs being done to my people." And when he followed by asking to what wrongs she referred, she started to list them without hesitation:

1. Removing us from our homelands.
2. Giving us no say in how our allotment money is spent.
3. Breaking treaties we have signed in good faith.
4. Providing no educational facilities for our children.

At this point the reporter cut her off and asked what she wanted the government to do. She answered with dignity, "First, I want that we be given a hearing. The government pays no attention to our requests. I want them first to listen and then to act."

After the reporter had closed his notebook and departed, Susette told Tibbles that she dreaded to see what would be in his paper about her the following day. When the story appeared the following day, it was a pleasant surprise. The reporter had described Susette (calling her Bright Eyes) as "petite, refined, intelligent," and he had quoted her accurately. It was hard to believe.

Ponca chief Standing Bear

Chapter 8

TRAGIC NEWS

With their commitments met in Chicago, the tour group was off to Pittsburgh. In this second city, things were going much as they had in Chicago until disaster fell on the little group. Susette was still panicky before each public appearance, but pretty and petite as well as dignified and sincere, she was able to win her audiences. Everything was in control for the foursome until two telegrams reached them.

The telegrams struck like a tornado. One was for Standing Bear with the message that his brother, Big Snake, had been killed in the territory. The other, even more devastating, was for Tibbles. It too bore a message of death: His wife had died. By the time the telegram reached him, her funeral had already been held.

Tibbles was grief-stricken. Susette had met Tibbles' wife Amelia and his two little girls when last in Omaha. She saw the tragic situation all too clearly. Besides the grief at losing his wife and the worry about what was to become of his girls, Susette knew there was guilt tearing him apart: guilt because he had left a substantial job, with money coming in regularly with which to support his family. He also felt guilty because he had left his wife to cope with raising their children alone, while he was off on a "crusade" for the Indians, a crusade that brought him travel, challenges, excitement, and satisfaction. Had Amelia opposed his going? But whether she had fought his decision or docilely accepted it, his guilt at leaving her was now bound to be overwhelming. Susette's sympathy for him was complete, but she was terribly concerned about what this tragedy would mean to their mission. Without Tibbles' guiding hand, what were they to do?

In the days that followed, with Tibbles too grief-stricken to leave his bed, she gained a little more information about Amelia's death. She had suffered a ruptured appendix and died of peritonitis, the acute inflammation of the membrane covering the stomach, intestines, and other organs of the abdomen. Bishop Clarkson, the same one who had arranged the Omaha lecture, had done another good deed. He had taken the two little Tibbles girls under his protection and had enrolled them in a private boarding school for girls in Omaha. This should give Tibbles some comfort, Susette thought, but neither this nor anything she could say roused him. Just when she was getting desperate, Standing Bear said the right thing to their leader to get him back on his feet. "Promise me," he said, "that you will not desert my people." Tibbles had promised, and again they were on their way.

It was not easy to get back to work, but with added effort they managed to complete their engagements in Pittsburgh. Susette's stage fright did not abate, but she was learning to put on a good performance in spite of it.

The next city on their agenda was Philadelphia. Knowledgeable about the city's historic significance, Susette looked forward to their time there. Also, each move eastward meant she was getting closer to New Jersey and Marguerite and Susan. She hoped to get a few days off to pay a visit to them soon. She was homesick for her family and the reservation. Letters were difficult to come by when they were traveling. Rosalie had managed to reach her with one letter, but it had only made her more homesick.

The letter was full of Rosalie's wedding plans, and Susette felt a twinge of envy. She knew that her family had thought of her as the old maid sister, the oldest of the four girls and still unmarried. It was expected that Omaha girls would marry, and Susette's family undoubtedly had worried about what was to become of her. She had at times herself wondered about her fate. There had been one handsome youth who had shown an interest in her, but she had given him no encouragement and he had taken another Indian maiden for his bride. Had she done the wrong thing in turning him away? Why had she felt that there was something important that she was to do with her life? Something to help her people? (Perhaps it was only because Iron Eye had made it so clear by word and by deed that their race would be lost if they did not take strong measures to adjust to the white people's ways, but at the same time to stand up for their rights.) She had tried teaching, but perhaps that had not been enough. Now she was trying this new thing, lecturing. She hoped it was what she was meant to do. It was hard, but if it did what Tibbles believed it would do, she would not complain.

Rosalie, besides telling of her wedding plans in her letter, said that Marguerite and Susan were doing well at school. Susan, she said, wrote long letters home telling of their activities and progress in their studies. The letters showed plainly that their sister Susan had lost none of her liveliness. Hearing about her little sisters made her all the more impatient to get to visit them at Elizabeth.

As Tibbles worked setting up their schedule in Philadelphia, Susette and Frank went to visit some of the historic places she had read about. They toured Constitution Hall and Independence Hall. They gazed in awe at the Liberty Bell. Susette reveled in the liberty the colonies had fought for and won. She realized that she was thinking as a white American. But when evening came and she stood before an audience, she would be introduced as the Indian maiden Bright Eyes, and she would think as an Indian as she presented her speech. The confusion of identities struck her again.

As she was dressing for one of her appearances, Frank brought her word of the delivery of another telegram. After the horror of the last two telegrams, news of another was frightening. However, Frank said this one did not have bad news. Mr. Tibbles wanted them all to be together and then he would read it to them.

Susette hurried her dressing and joined the others. But she did not anticipate how good the news in this telegram was to be. Tibbles kept them in suspense. Before he read the telegram, he told them it contained evidence that their tour was getting results, that they now had "the first fruits of their labor." Finally he broke the suspense. He read the telegram aloud:

BILL TO REMOVE OMAHAS TO INDIAN TERRITORY DEFEATED BY CONGRESS.

This was joy beyond belief. As they rejoiced together, Susette unexpectedly called Tibbles "T.H." T.H. stood for Thomas Henry, and the initials were used as a first name. Almost everyone called him T.H., but Susette had always called him Mr. Tibbles. She did not realize until later when she was alone in her room that she had addressed him by the more familiar term.

Thomas Henry "T.H." Tibbles

Chapter 9

AUTHORS AHOY!

From then on Susette called Tibbles "T.H." After all, he had addressed her as "Bright Eyes" ever since they had left home. Her feelings for this white person with whom she was traveling had changed somewhat in the weeks they had been on tour. At first she had felt a little resentment toward him. She didn't like the way he had given orders. It was almost as if he were trying to take over Iron Eye's place. But either his grief had mellowed him a bit or her sympathy for him had made her less critical. At any rate she felt more friendly toward him than she had at the outset of their pilgrimage.

The trip from Philadelphia to their next engagement in Boston began well, with what Tibbles referred to as another "good telegram." It was from the Boston Indian Committee, and it pertained to Susette. It said that area authors were eager to meet Bright Eyes and that parties were being planned for the purpose of introducing her. T.H. was very pleased with this, but Susette, seeing it as another new and therefore frightening experience, was not. She supposed it was nice that people wanted to meet her, but she didn't understand why authors would consider it a privilege, she told T.H. He thought the way the press had been profiling her as "a beautiful Indian

45

maiden" had appealed to the authors as "romantic," and, he said, authors loved the romantic.

Just thinking about the parties to come made Susette nervous. However, as things worked out, her first experience was a pleasant one. It was a private dinner party where only one author was present—the poet Henry Wadsworth Longfellow. Susette had read his poetry including the poem "Hiawatha," about an Indian woman named Minnehaha which Susette had loved.

On the night of the party Susette was experiencing her usual attack of shyness. However, when she was ushered into the room where the poet sat, the shyness left her, for he sprang to his feet with a big smile and outstretched hands. "My Minnehaha," he said, taking both of her hands in his. Before the evening was over, he had presented her with a copy of the poem "Hiawatha." The next party was a much larger one with guests including musicians and artists as well as authors.

Shortly after this a story appeared in a local paper about Susette and her activities in Boston. It referred to her as "the Indian Princess Bright Eyes." This seemed to have instigated the biggest party of all, one given by the distinguished publisher Houghton.

Susette expressed the hope that she might meet Louisa May Alcott. She did. She also met Ralph Waldo Emerson, an essayist whose work she admired; another poet, John Greenleaf Whittier; and Helen Hunt Jackson, who was to become a good friend and a strong voice for the Indian cause.

When Susette was introduced to Louisa May Alcott, she said, "Oh, I was so hoping I would meet you. I'm very fond of your book *Little Women*."

Miss Alcott responded with thanks, but then went on to say that there was someone present whom she wanted Susette to meet. This was Mary Mapes Dodge, editor of the children's magazine *St. Nicholas*.

When the meeting took place, Mrs. Mapes had a surprising offer for Susette. She said she would like to have her write a little story for *St. Nicholas*, something out of her own child-hood. Susette explained that the only writing she had done had been newspaper stories, helping Mr. Tibbles. Mrs. Dodge nonetheless repeated her request, and so Susette had promised to try to write a story for her.

Not only was Susette winning wide acclaim as a guest at celebrity parties, she also was much in demand for speaking engagements other than her scheduled ones. One noon, by special request, she addressed five hundred businessmen in downtown Boston. Newspaper stories were claiming that not since colonial days and the Boston Tea Party had Boston been so aroused over a cause. Money was pouring into their coffers, Tibbles reported. And the pressure of the aroused citizens of the highly respected city of Boston was being felt in Washington.

Susette was beginning to tire, with her heavy schedule of

both day and evening activities, and had asked how much longer their extended stay in Boston was to last, when an unexpected request came for her to speak in Faneuil Hall. This was a great honor, as she was the first woman ever asked to speak there.

She fulfilled this duty, winning her usual personal acclaim, but also much sympathy and strong support not only for the Poncas, but for all of the other tribes of the Western Plains, referred to as the Plains Indians.

CHAPTER 10

"LAW IS LIBERTY"

The year 1878 was almost over. It was December before what had come to be known as "The Indian Party" moved on to New York. Before they left Boston, Susette had sent off a little story to *St. Nicholas* magazine. She called it "Nedawi."

As they had done so well gaining financial support while in Boston, Susette asked if it would be possible, when they reached New York, for her to have a couple of days off to visit Marguerite and Susan at Elizabeth Institute. Tibbles agreed that while they were this close she should have some time with her sisters. Also, he thought a little time off would be good for her, giving her some rest from her rigorous schedule.

When she arrived at Elizabeth, she was given a reception fitting the role of "Indian Princess," which she had won in Boston. A gala party had been planned by Miss Read, the same headmistress as in Susette's days there. She and the teachers were extremely proud of this famous graduate.

What Susette had come for, however, was a visit with Marguerite and Susan. It was difficult to find time alone with them, and when she did, it was not entirely satisfactory. The girls seemed a bit awed at the celebrity their sister had become. And most of their conversation took the form of pleading for the chance to go home for Rosalie's wedding. Susette explained to them that she had no money, that Tibbles was in charge of the group's finances and that all the money they took in went for the expenses of their daily living and their travel.

The money was not for personal use. Still, seeing their elder sister well dressed, poised, and adored, it was hard for the younger sisters to accept this. When Susette left after her short visit, she felt dissatisfied with the time that she had looked forward to so eagerly. There were disadvantages to being a famous person.

But at least she had seen that her sisters were well adjusted in the white world into which they had been thrust. They not only were accepted by their classmates; they were popular with them. And scholastically they were doing well. Susan, the better student of the two, was excelling in every subject, and Marguerite was making her grades.

Also it had been good getting news from home. Her sisters kept in touch through letters between Susan and Rosalie. Both Mary and Nicomi had been ill but were recovering. Susan went into a tirade about their people not knowing how to take care of themselves and about the need for medical assistance on the reservation. She said too that Iron Eye was badly in need of a new wooden leg. She knew this was true because Rosalie said the stump of his leg was paining him seriously.

Rosalie's report about herself, Susan had said, had to do with wedding plans. She had talked to Father William Hamilton and he would conduct the ceremony for her and Ed at the old mission church. She was planning a June wedding, and Nicomi, Mary, and she were making her dress. It was to be a white dress such as they had seen in pictures, the kind white women wore for their weddings.

Back in New York, Susette was soon caught up in her old routine. She did not have as many social engagements as she had had in Boston, but her platform appearances were well received, and the newspapers were giving the Indian Party good coverage.

They would of course be in New York for a number of weeks—longer than at their other stops—due to the size of the city. But after New York, what? Tibbles said they would probably either be returning to Philadelphia or be going to Washington, D.C.

They might be called to the capital as witnesses in the hearings that were going on about the Poncas. There were heated debates about what was to be done with them. Should they be forced to remain in the Indian Territory, or should their lands on the Niobrara be restored to them? Tibbles was sure that the Eastern cities' favorable reaction to their lecture tour was having its effect on Congress and the government agencies involved with the Indians.

For some time Tibbles had been working on a book that he intended to have published under a pseudonym. He was calling it *The Ponca Chiefs*, and he had asked Susette to write the introduction for the book. This she did, and included in it she wrote the sentence, "Law is liberty." This was to be much quoted in the future.

Working closely with T.H. on this writing project, Susette began to realize that she had developed a certain fondness for him. Before the book went to press, she learned that this feeling was mutual. T.H. asked her to marry him.

Chapter 11

"NEDAWI"

Susette did not accept T.H's offer of marriage at once. She wanted time to think about what it would mean. There was the matter of Tibbles' two little girls to consider, Eda and May, whom Susette had met only once. What kind of stepmother would she make? Then there was Rosalie's wedding, just a few months away. Susette hoped to be able to return home for it, and she would not want an announcement of her wedding to dim the luster of Rosalie's.

While the Indian Party was still in New York, Susette received a letter that she hurried to share with T.H. It was from the *St. Nicholas* magazine and to her surprise and delight, it contained a check. Her story "Nedawi" was to appear in the January issue of the magazine.

What especially delighted Susette was the fact that the check gave her a little money of her own. Christmas was very near, and it would be wonderful to be able to send some gifts to her family on the reservation and to Marguerite and Susan at Elizabeth.

In January, the group returned to Philadelphia, and from then on spent frantic, wearying months going back and forth between that city and Washington. Susette became so accustomed to giving testimony in regard to the Poncas that a call from Washington no longer frightened her.

On the train during one of these trips between cities, a Mrs. Hemenway made herself known to Susette and T.H. After visiting with them for a time she said, looking at Susette, that she thought they deserved and needed a rest. She hoped to see that they got it.

Not long after they were at work again in Philadelphia, they received a wire from the Boston Indian Committee. Ever their staunchest supporter, Boston had come through. Reservations had been made for them at a spa for a week's vacation. Mrs. Hemenway had alerted the committee to their desperate need.

It was a much appreciated break, but for Susette a trip home was what she thought necessary for her to regain her energy. That trip came in time for her to attend Rosalie's wedding. There was reason for all three of the little group to take a vacation and to feel accomplishment, for the five-man Senate committee working on the Ponca situation had turned in its report. It was a unanimous one, saying that they believed the Poncas had been wrongfully treated by the U.S. government's action in removing them from their homeland to Indian Territory and that they deserved immediate redress.

The report was most rewarding, but it was only the first step. What they had to work for now was to see that a bill to restore the Poncas' lands was drawn up and presented to

Congress and, the ultimate goal, passed into law.

The completion of the Senate Committee's Ponca report brought relief to Standing Bear too. Before the party left the East for home, he told T.H. and Susette that he was through with testimonies and speeches. He also made a symbolic move to show that he was a person in the sight of the law. He had his long black braids cut off and came out of the barbershop with a stylish haircut of the day.

Back on the reservation, Susette was able to forget the life of protest that she had been living so intensely and devote herself to helping with Rosalie's wedding preparations. In the meantime, T.H. went off to the Indian Territory to see first-hand what present conditions were like for the Poncas.

Iron Eye expressed his appreciation to his eldest daughter for what she had done since leaving them, and this meant much to Susette. Even though she had received commendation from many people in high places, her father's gratitude was the most satisfying. He was the one who had been fore-sighted enough to start the Omahas on adjusting to the white world. He had seen that action must be taken to prevent the Indians from becoming mere puppets with white people pulling the strings.

She had great respect for her father. If he had not sent her to Elizabeth to get an education, she would not have been able to give her influential lectures, nor to meet important people and win them to the Indians' cause, nor to give telling testimony to the Senate Committee.

In the long view, though, Susette told her father, the goal was to get citizenship for Indians. Judge Dundy had started it with his decision that "An Indian is a person," but there was a long road ahead before they would be given citizenship. Her vacation could not be an extended one. Too much work lay ahead.

Much as Susette and Rosalie wanted their two younger sisters at Rosalie's wedding, there was simply no money with which to bring them home. Susette was the only La Flesche sister in attendance at the June wedding.

The Reverend Hamilton, affectionately called "Father" by the Omahas, who had stayed on at the reservation after the Presbyterian mission with which he was affiliated was officially closed, performed the Christian ceremony. Rosalie, at nineteen, was beautiful, an Indian maiden dressed as a white bride, taking a white woman's wedding vows, marrying a white man.

Although Susette did not foresee the importance of the role her sister had chosen for herself—that of remaining on the reservation—the potential was there and it would be realized. She would be an important instrument in helping her people adjust to the changes to come.

At the close of the ceremony, Susette placed her signature on the marriage certificate of Rosalie La Flesche and Edward Farley. This document, she thought, was proof that Iron Eye's assertion that Indians must learn to live as the whites lived was even now being observed.

Above: Rosalie La Flesche Farley
Below: Francis La Flesche

Above: Marguerite La Flesche Picotte Diddock
Below: Dr. Susan La Flesche Picotte

A 1914 photograph shows harvesting with eight horses. Jack Farley, grandson of Iron Eye, is shocking wheat.

Four of Iron Eye's granddaughters, about 1901

Left: A photograph taken approximately 1880 shows Susan La Flesche (standing) and Marguerite La Flesche (sitting on right).
Right: Edward Farley (Rosalie's husband) and their son, Eddie, Jr.

Francis "Bull Eagle" La Flesche

Below: Mr. and Mrs. Tibbles are seated on the right in this photo. Also included are Marjorie Diddock (standing), Carey La Flesche, and Miss Fremont, a distant cousin of Susette La Flesche Tibbles.

Left: Sitting in the 1884 class photograph of Hampton Institute, Virginia, are Josephine Barnaby, Marguerite La Flesche, and Charles F. Picotte. Marguerite and Charles were married in 1888.

Left: Susette Tibbles is in the center picture on the dresser in a bedroom in Dr. Susan La Flesche Picotte's house.
Right: Susan La Flesche Picotte's sons, Caryl, born in 1895, and Pierre, born in 1898

Alice Fletcher (left) and Francis La Flesche (right) were photographed at a Pageant of Lincoln in Omaha, Nebraska, in 1916.

The building in which Susette La Flesche taught school about 1877 to 1878

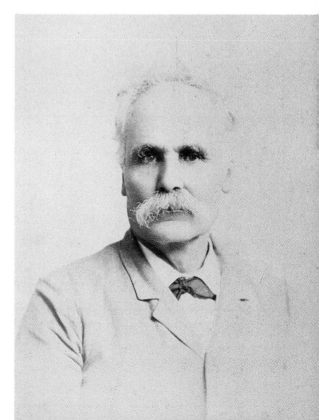

Portrait of
T.H. Tibbles

The Thomas H. Tibbles home in Lincoln, Nebraska, was furnished in a typical Victorian style. Drapes, throws, pillows, and photographs or portraits were common. There also is Indian handwork and beads on the curtains.

Chapter 12

A MEASURE OF SUCCESS

Susette went on the road again. Standing Bear's absence meant a difference in platform procedure, and the others missed his company, but their busy schedule forced them to adapt rapidly. Susette no longer told Standing Bear's emotion-packed story. She now put more emphasis on the larger picture of human rights and the need for Indians to be given citizenship.

As before, she was enthusiastically received. At times when she spoke in smaller facilities such as churches, people had to be turned away for lack of space. But there was the other side of the coin as well. At times there was bad press when the truth of her statements was questioned or she was criticized for playing upon people's emotions. So there was discouragement along with success, and progress seemed infinitely slow.

Hence it was almost with disbelief that they heard in March that the bill pertaining to the Poncas' lands had reached the floor of the Senate and debate was under way. Then it seemed that the debate would never end. The closing date of the session was drawing near. But finally, on the very last day before it ended, the bill was brought to a vote.

Susette and T.H. waited in almost unbearable suspense for a wire telling them the outcome of the vote. When it came, it brought relief and jubilation. The telegram said simply, "THE AYES HAVE IT!" The long months of grueling labor had at last brought results! The recommendations of the Senate Committee before which Susette and T.H. had testified were largely followed. The provisions of the bill were as follows:

All of their old reservation on the Niobrara was to be restored to the Poncas.

Each man now in Indian Territory could choose whether to remain or return to the reservation.

The Poncas would be reimbursed for their goods that had been taken when they were moved.

Their homes on the reservation were to be repaired and restored.

Schools would be established.

$50,000 would be provided for the return of those wishing to leave the territory and return to the reservation.

In all of this Susette and T.H. rejoiced, but best of all was the fact that the Poncas' land would be restored to them. And didn't this success prove that the Indians were finally being listened to? It was a red-letter day not only for Susette and T.H., but also for the many people who had backed their efforts.

Chapter 13

WEDDING VOWS

Besides the enactment of the Ponca Bill, there were other bright spots in Susette's world. One of these was the people she had met who had taken up the Indian cause with vigor. Among those whom she particularly enjoyed was Helen Hunt Jackson, who was working on an Indian story she was calling *Ramona*, a tragic romance of Indian injustice.

Then in Washington there was Alice Fletcher, an anthropologist who was very much interested in studying the Omaha tribe. She wanted to visit their reservation and had struck up a friendship with Frank. Such friends often worked as hard for the Indian cause as Susette herself, and with telling results.

The year 1880 came to a close with Tibbles pressing Susette for marriage. She had given him her promise, but she saw no need for haste. The two of them had become close in their work together, which included considerable writing. She had helped him with two books, both propaganda for improving the Indian situation, and he had plans for others. He found Susette of great help both because of her keen intellect and because of her thorough knowledge of the Plains Indians.

Susette wanted to be married on the reservation as Rosalie had been. Sometime in 1881, she promised T.H. In the meantime, there was work to do. At times when she was tired or discouraged, she would get out one of her autograph books and read from it. Many friends had written heart-warming messages, and these she cherished, but the ones she went back to most often were those written by people who had been only acquaintances but had substantially helped her cause. She had barely met the two attorneys who had obtained the writ of habeas corpus for Standing Bear. Yet Attorney John Webster had written:

The Law shall soon come to know the rights of the Indian race, and the Indian race to feel the benefi-cence of the Law.

This she prized. It was written and signed in his clear, round hand, and it made Susette a believer: The Indian race *would* know the kindly hand of the law, though the time of waiting was long.

As spring came, Susette confided in her family and her close friends that she and T.H. were planning to be married in July. The reply from the reservation was joyous. The La Flesche family was relieved and delighted that the eldest daughter was at last to be married. Rosalie wrote of her especial joy in the announcement. She was so happy married to Ed, and she was sure Susette would find a new happiness with T.H. She had news too. She and Ed were going to have a baby, and this would make her life complete.

Some of Susette's Boston friends, delighted with her news,

insisted that they supply her wedding dress. It proved to be beautiful, made of soft challis, spilling with ruffles, and trimmed in exquisite lace. The lace formed a stand-up collar, cuffed the long sleeves, and fell in a panel the full length of the skirt. The skirt was draped at the sides and caught up at the back into wide flounces that extended into a graceful train. Admiring it gratefully, she still thought it looked more fitting for a young white socialite than for the shy young Indian woman whom her soon-to-be-husband called Bright Eyes.

She had to laugh as she examined the clustered flounces in the back, for they reminded her of the first time she and her uncle had seen women in the East wearing bustles. Standing Bear had said they looked like overgrown turkeys!

The wedding was to take place in the same little mission church where Rosalie's had been held, but Father Hamilton was not to conduct the ceremony. He and Iron Eye were in the midst of a heated dispute, and Iron Eye asked Susette to get another minister. The Reverend S.N.D. Martin, missionary to another Indian tribe, the Winnebagos, would perform the rite.

Years later, writing his autobiography, T.H. said, "Bright Eyes and I were married at the old Presbyterian mission on the Omaha Reservation in the great building erected there by Rev. William Hamilton about 1854. That building was a picturesque building of 'grout,' as the mixture of sand, lime, and stone was called, and stood on the bank of the Missouri River in a great forest."

Frank was the only member of the La Flesche family not attending Susette's wedding. The new secretary of the interior, the same Senator Kirkwood of the Senate Committee before which the Indian Party had testified, remembered Frank's ability as an interpreter and had given him a position in the Bureau of Indian Affairs. Marguerite and Susan, to their delight, had been able to return home for the summer and so were able to attend this wedding.

Chapter 14

VISIT TO STANDING BEAR

There would be no opportunity for Susette and T.H. to set up a proper home at this time, for they were soon to return East for yet another lecture tour, their third. And in the meantime, Alice Fletcher, the anthropologist with whom they had become friends in the East, had finally persuaded T.H. to set up a study tour for her, an "exploration" on the Omaha reservation. This promise had to be fulfilled before he and Susette set out. T.H. had tried to discourage Miss Fletcher by telling her they would have to camp out, live in a tent, and endure hardships, but he had not succeeded.

Alice Fletcher arrived in Omaha by train a couple of months after Susette and Tibbles' marriage. The fall rains had started early, and the couple, who had planned to initiate Miss Fletcher into Indian ways by camping out en route to the reservation, looked with some trepidation to the lowering clouds as her train pulled in. They had prepared well with tents, blankets, cooking utensils, and food, but it was not good weather for camping, especially for one with no experience in roughing it. Miss Fletcher nevertheless insisted that they carry out their plans. Before they reached the reservation, T.H. took back all his remarks about how this "tenderfoot" would be ready to return to Washington on the first train. She won the respect both of him and of Susette as she took rain and mud and cold with good humor. Susette's fondness and admiration for her only increased on their miserable trip to the reservation.

Once they arrived on the reservation, Miss Fletcher began visiting Omaha families, with Susette interpreting for her. At first, Susette noted, the visitor asked no questions, but she was a keen observer. A little later after one of her hosts asked point blank why she was on the reservation, she explained, through Susette, that she wanted to learn about the Omahas' history and customs. She was very interested. From then on, the Omahas were eager to explain their rituals and to sing their songs for her. From this they went on to tell her how much their land meant to them and how they thought they should have some title to the portions they had homesteaded. Alice Fletcher listened.

Susette agreed that her people should have titles to the plots of land they had developed, and since the Ponca situation no longer required her attention, this was one of the things for which she had been campaigning. It was referred to as "land in Severalty," meaning land owned by individuals.

Now Alice Fletcher started asking the Omahas to bring her any papers they had regarding what piece of land they had been living on and farming. She told Susette insistently that it was time something was done to ensure the Indians' right to their land. They should get this urgent message to Congress.

A severalty bill should be introduced. Susette promised to begin working on it as soon as she and T.H. went East again.

Alice Fletcher also brought news about a school in Hampton, Virginia, which she thought would soon have possibilities for the young men who wanted to learn better ways of farming. It was called Hampton Institute and had been established at the close of the Civil War for blacks. Now they were considering opening it to Indians as well.

Susan happened to be present at the time Alice Fletcher was telling about Hampton, and she began asking eager questions about the school. Miss Fletcher explained that it was for young men only. Susan protested that women should be given as much chance at education as men. Miss Fletcher took note of Susan's interest. Here was another La Flesche daughter who gave evidence of her father's influence and would perhaps find a way to help her tribe in their difficult transition period.

There was one more service Susette and T.H. had promised to perform for Alice Fletcher before they started East again. It would mean far more camping out than their brief experience with roughing it when she first arrived. This was something Susette and T.H. were looking forward to on their own account. It was a trip to the Niobrara to visit Standing Bear and the Poncas who had returned to their homeland.

The three set out in a light spring wagon pulled by two ponies, and accompanied by Wajapa, their guide, riding a third pony. The journey would take them on a northerly trail of over a hundred miles as the crow flies. It was a rugged trip on which they encountered rainstorms, hot winds, and breakdowns with the wagon.

Wajapa gave Miss Fletcher an Indian name, which Susette found difficult to translate into English. "High Flyer," she said was as near as she could come. They all thought it a good name for Alice Fletcher, so two Indian names, High Flyer and Bright Eyes, resounded over the prairies on the long trek. There were beautiful days when the weather cooperated; there were wild animals to watch; there were cozy nights around the campfire.

At long last, they found the Poncas, and Standing Bear greeted them with such joy that they were touched. Some rainy days followed, during which they enjoyed the hospitality of their host's tent. They were valuable hours for Alice Fletcher as she filled her notebook with stories of the Poncas' earlier days, their dances, their ceremonies. Valuable too for Susette, a renewing experience, for it was like being back in her childhood.

Chapter 15

EAST AGAIN

The satisfying visit to the Poncas was over. It was time for Susette and T.H. to go East again. An aunt of T.H's daughters had been caring for the girls, but now T.H. arranged for them to enter boarding school again. Until he and Susette could be in one place long enough to establish a home, it seemed the best solution. Susette had sensed a coolness toward her on the part of Eda and May when they had been in her presence. When the time did come for a home for the four of them, it did not promise to be an easy situation.

Marguerite and Susan were returning to Elizabeth Institute for their last year. Rosalie was reveling in her family. She had a little girl now and was pregnant again. And Frank was well pleased with his job in Washington.

After months of hard work, Alice Fletcher had her petition for land allotments for the Omahas prepared. She was going to send it to a member of Congress of her acquaintance in whom she had considerable confidence. The petition was accompanied by the signatures (their marks) of fifty-five Omahas, the number of acres each cultivated, the stock owned, and the number of dependents.

Now Susette would make the thrust of her lectures pertain

to the need for a land allotment bill that would give her people some feeling of permanence and more reason to work the land and strive to raise better crops. But along with this she would not forget the all-important cause of Indian citizenship.

Again when they reached the Eastern cities, Susette was widely entertained. She had made many friends on her previous tours, all of whom were eager to entertain for her when she was available.

T.H. was as enthusiastic as ever about their work for the Indians. He was writing another book concerning their causes, and Susette was editing it. Over and over he said that they must not rest on their success with the Poncas. They must keep up the fight until the government changed its whole policy toward the Indians.

Not only was Susette editing T.H's writing, she was doing more of her own. Having found a way to help white children understand the Indian race, she wrote more stories about Indian children, which found their way into children's magazines. The writing success she was having added to her popularity among Eastern authors, especially in Boston. Edward Everett Hale, a Harvard-educated minister and writer, who had become famous for a story he had written in 1863 called *The Man Without a Country*, was much taken with Susette. He saw to it that she met Eastern authors and other notables and arranged parties in her honor. She had begun illustrating her stories with little sketches of Indian life, and these added further appeal to "the Indian Princess Bright Eyes."

Delightful news came in a letter from Rosalie. Susan had been notified that she had the highest grades in her class and would be graduated from Elizabeth in the spring with top honors. The girls would be home on the reservation by summer. T.H. was planning that he and Susette would end their tour by that time also. Susette, who was getting very tired again, could hardly wait for summer.

Before the longed-for vacation time came, another piece of good news reached them. The senator to whom Alice Fletcher had sent the petition for Omaha land allotments had notified her that he had approved the petition and had presented it to a Congressional Committee. Susette's push now was for a bill following the lines of the petition to be drafted and sent to Congress. That must be the next step. And then a law!

And always there was her plea for Indian citizenship. Still, her lectures no longer drew the immense crowds of the earlier years, though the attendance was always respectable. All in all, T.H. thought it was time to go home.

Going home was going to be different for Mrs. T.H. Tibbles than it had been for Susette La Flesche. She would be living in the city of Omaha rather than on the reservation. She would be living in Amelia Tibbles' house, surrounded by Amelia's things. And most different of all, there would be two young girls living in that house with her and T.H.

It did not prove to be easy, but she tried very hard. She put out her books and told Eda and May they were free to use them. She told them stories of what her life had been like when she was their age. And she talked to them often of the life she had led with their father on tour, stressing how wonderful it had been for him to give up so much for the Indian cause. They had a father to be proud of! She tried to give them helpful suggestions for their own lives, always being careful not to dictate. But whatever she did, she felt the girls remained distant. Yet years later, a letter written by Eda said they had loved and admired their stepmother.

Susette and T.H. waited eagerly for news of a land allotment's bill going to Congress, but they waited in vain. Again, as in other times of discouragement, Susette would turn to her autograph albums. There was a new inscription which she prized particularly. It was signed "George Crook, Brig. General, U.S.A."—the general they had fought for Standing Bear's freedom. It read, "Bright Eyes has accomplished more for the benefit of her race than their combined effort within my recollection." This was good to read, but at present she was accomplishing nothing except through her writing and the editing of T.H.'s latest book, *A Century of Dishonor.*

With the publication of Helen Hunt Jackson's novel *Ramona,* things looked brighter. The book was an instant success, and even though fiction, the stirring story touched people's hearts and would undoubtedly do great good for the Indian cause.

Chapter 16

DOUBLE SUCCESS

After what seemed forever to those involved, a bill to give the Omahas allotments of land did reach Congress, and once there, passed quickly into law. And wonder of wonders, it included a clause giving citizenship to those who accepted allotments. Susette reveled in this double success.

More good news followed. Alice Fletcher was appointed special agent to see the provisions of the law carried out. It would be good to have her back on the reservation. When she did get there, it was an exciting time. The mood of the Omahas was jubilant, that of the La Flesche family at a peak of joy and pride.

Alice Fletcher had brought good news of a different nature. The Hampton Institute had opened its doors to women, and she thought Marguerite and Susan would be good candidates for entrance. The courses for women were to prepare them to teach. Would the girls be interested? They were thrilled with the thought of further education, and Marguerite was sure she would like to become a teacher. Susan was not sure that this was what she wanted for her future but would be delighted to get more education.

Before the initial steps of finding sponsors for the girls

and applying for admission were taken, there was a formidable obstacle to be met in Iron Eye. Susette, remembering her father's objection to her going on tour with two men, was sure he would object to his daughters attending a coeducational school.

When Alice Fletcher approached him with the possibility of further education for Marguerite and Susan, he was very pleased. The more education his children could get, the better. But when she told him that courses for men were in agriculture and for women in teacher training, it was a different story. Of course he would not send his daughters to a school where there were men students. Why would she even suggest it?

Susette was there to back up her friend, emphasizing the value to the tribe if the girls could teach on the reservation, and pointing out that coeducational schools were common in the white people's world, the world to which he said they must adjust.

In the end, Iron Eye gave in, Marguerite and Susan rejoiced, and Alice Fletcher set about to get them enrolled. Another period of waiting followed. Susette thought the Omahas did more waiting than anything else.

Her wait for a plot of ground on which T.H. could build them a house was not as long, however, as many she had endured. With Alice Fletcher handling the allotments, hers came through in good time. Susette would be so very happy to live on the reservation again. But there were matters to be taken care of before this could come about. Finances were at a low ebb for the Tibbles family. They had returned from their last trip East with virtually no money. It was scarcely a time for house building.

Good news came for the younger La Flesche sisters before the summer was out. Miss Fletcher had found sponsors who would finance them at Hampton. Now all that remained was to get them admitted.

Susette, in visiting with Alice Fletcher, learned that Frank was working with her on her study of the Omaha culture. This was a project that would take years to complete, for Alice wanted it to include every aspect of the tribe's organization, rites, religion, social life, language, music, and dance. It was a matter of great pride to Susette that Frank was playing an important part in this work.

Barely in time to reach Hampton, Virginia, for the opening of the winter term of the Institute, Marguerite and Susan received word that they had been granted admission. It was a time of great rejoicing.

A photograph taken in approximately 1889 shows Edward and Rosalie Farley and some of their children.

Chapter 17

LIVING LIKE WHITES

But it also was a time of tension for Susette. T.H. was restless, with no tours on the agenda and no big projects to take his attention. The education of Eda and May was a problem. There was simply no money to send them to preparatory school in Lincoln, Nebraska, which was their ambition.

But at least Susette was to have a house of her own, which was a great relief. During the summer T.H. had started to build one for her, a small "soddy." Now it was taking shape. It wasn't much, but it would be her own, on her own land, representing a small portion of what she and T.H. had fought for. Then a place was found in Lincoln where Eda and May, now young teenagers, could work for their board and room and attend school. Things looked better.

On the reservation all was going well for the La Flesche family. Rosalie, in addition to her little daughter, now had twin boys. She was busy and happy with her family plus helping Ed on a big project. He had taken a twenty-year lease on a large area of grazing land that had not gone for land allotments. It was excellent pasture, and after fencing it, he rented it out to farmers, both Indians and whites, who were in need of grazing land for their cattle. The business was going very well, and

Rosalie was both bookkeeper and go-between. With her ability to use both the Omaha language and English, she was able to make explanations to renters when problems or misunderstandings arose. More and more Susette could see that Rosalie's position during this time of transition for the Indians was a very valuable one. Word from Hampton indicated that Marguerite and Susan were not only doing well with their studies, but that they were also enjoying the social life that the school afforded: coeducational opportunities, with parties and church-related activities bringing the young men and women together. Marguerite's letters were now filled with praises of a young man named Charles Picotte. And before long Susan told of her being singled out by a youth who, she wrote, was "the handsomest Indian I've ever seen." His name was Thomas Ikinicapi. He was called "T.I."

The summer after Susette and T.H. moved into their little sod house, T.H. tried to farm Susette's land. It was not a successful attempt. T.H. was not the type to follow a plow with any degree of satisfaction. It was thus no surprise to Susette when one day he said he believed he would contact a booking agent to see if he could line up a speaking tour for the two of them in England. It seemed an unlikely possibility, but if a more suitable occupation than farming could be found for T.H., it would be well. Also, they could certainly use some money. T.H's struggling farm operation was not making them a decent living. As difficult as lecturing had always been for her,

Susette thought she would welcome a bit of that old life.

From time to time, T.H. received requests for their appearance in short-term engagements in Eastern cities. These were most welcome. In lectures now, it was the story of their successes that Susette told, from getting Standing Bear released from jail and the Indian declared "a person" with the right to be heard in court, through getting the Poncas' lands back for them, the Allotment Bill passed, and citizenship for Omahas who had taken land allotments. This she followed with her biggest plea ever—for citizenship for all Indians. At times it seemed unlikely that this would ever come about, but T.H. and Alice Fletcher both insisted that it would. So the year 1885 came to a close. In the eight years since Standing Bear had struggled toward "home" with the bones of his son, the Plains Indians had largely succeeded in doing what Iron Eye had said they must: adjust to the white people's way of life. It had not been easy blending the old ways with the new, but out of necessity it had been done.

The Tibbles house on Susette's allotment north of Bancroft

Chapter 18

NEW CHALLENGE

The year 1886 was to be an eventful year for Susette and her sisters. As Susette had anticipated, news from Hampton indicated that both Marguerite's and Susan's interest in certain young men had ripened. In fact, Marguerite's had reached the point of an engagement to Charles Picotte. No such news came from Susan, however. Her letters left no doubt about her love for Thomas Ikinicapi, but she had plans other than marriage for her immediate future. She was applying for admission to the Women's Medical College in Philadelphia. Inspired by all Susette had done for their people, Susan wanted to become a doctor and return to the reservation to care for the Omahas' physical needs. Marguerite, who had missed much school because of illness, would have to return to Hampton the following year to complete requirements for graduation.

Susan was the salutatorian of her graduating class and at commencement would give an address titled "My Childhood and My Womanhood." The best news of all was word that Susan had been accepted for medical college. No one was much surprised, perhaps Alice Fletcher least of all. The previous summer, suffering from a severe case of rheumatic fever, she had been nursed by Susan. Susan had shown a great interest and skill in medical matters.

In the fall, when Susan was already in Philadelphia, Susette and T.H. were asked to do some lecturing in New York, so they had the opportunity to visit Susan. Susette was very proud that her little sister was in medical school. Susan, equally proud of Susette, whose reputation was well known in Philadelphia, was pleased when colleagues asked if Susette would speak at one of their meetings. T.H. was opposed to her doing so as he thought she was already weary from the speeches she had been making, but she insisted. Anything her little sister asked of her she would do. She realized that Susan had given up love for this career, the ultimate aim of which was to help her people. While she herself had devoted her life to their betterment, she had T.H.

Marguerite had married Charles Picotte, a Sioux whom she had met in school at Hampton, and was back on the reservation teaching. Rosalie, still bearing children, was not only a source of advice to many members of the tribe who brought their troubles to her, but also a great help to the poor and the ill. Susette and her sisters and her brother were all active in fulfilling their father's hopes and dreams for the Omahas.

Back in New York, but soon to return to the reservation, Susette and T.H. were staying in a hotel while T.H. completed some business details. While he was out, Susette was resting. Suddenly she was startled by T.H. bursting into the room, as excited and exuberant as he had been in the peak days of their crusade. He had great news, he shouted. He had found an agent who would set up a tour for them in England and Scotland!

So they actually were going abroad! It was almost unbelievable. In 1886, to cross the ocean? And she an Indian! What were their lectures to be about? The agent had said simply, "About the American Indian." That left them lots of leeway. But wouldn't it be hard to break through the British reserve? Susette wondered. And would audiences abroad really be interested in the American Indian?

T.H. assured her that her beauty and charm would break through any reserve. And if the English and Scottish people weren't interested in the American Indian before, they would be after they met his Bright Eyes. T.H. was his old lively self again.

So they returned home to prepare for their last big speaking tour. Such a venture seemed to Susette's family to be too much for T.H. to ask of Susette. They did not always approve of Thomas Tibbles with his big ideas and enthusiasm. But the plans and preparations went on apace.

A portrait of Susette La Flesche Tibbles

Chapter 19

A YEAR ABROAD

It was May of the following year before Susette and T.H. set sail for England. A manager accompanied them. Almost as soon as they arrived in London, the manager deserted them. He had found an American theatrical troupe that he preferred to manage rather than their lecture tour. This was a serious blow, but luckily T.H. had done some thoughtful preparation for the trip. He had secured letters of introduction and commendation from a number of their supporters in the Eastern cities. He had turned particularly to Boston and well-known authors from that area. Such names he was sure would be meaningful abroad.

Now in London without a manager, he turned to the letters. He chose one from James Russell Lowell, a well-known American poet, to a Presbyterian minister by the name of Fraser. With high hopes, he proceeded to the minister's study and presented it. The letter, however, did not bring the results he had hoped for—an invitation for Susette to speak at the Reverend Fraser's church. Instead, with the slightest of smiles the minister shook his head. Women were not permitted to speak in the churches of his denomination in England.

Weighed down with the defeat of his first attempt to get

Susette and himself out of their serious predicament, T.H. stopped at a couple of booking agencies before returning to give Susette the bad news. To his surprise, he found her in high spirits. She said she had an exciting story to tell. A very nice gentleman had come to call on her. They had such a pleasant visit. Then he had asked her to speak at his church the following Sunday evening. Wasn't that remarkable?

Even more remarkable to Tibbles was the card the gentleman had left. It bore the name and address of the minister on whom he had just called. A visit with Susette had obviously been more convincing than his plea.

Susette spoke at Dr. Fraser's church and was cordially received. Following her lecture, Reverend Fraser himself introduced her to many of his parishioners, calling her Bright Eyes. There were many titles among the people whom she met.

Although impressed with meeting members of royal families, Susette objected to herself being considered royalty. She protested a newspaper story in which, as of old, she was referred to as "the Indian Princess Bright Eyes."

Soon after her appearance at Dr. Fraser's church, the Tibbles had a new manager. After the article about her appeared, a London booking agency contacted T.H. and arrangements were made for a local agent.

Although this manager worked out satisfactorily, the "royalty" problem almost brought disaster. The manager had pamphlets printed advertising Susette's lectures, and in them she was again referred to as "the Indian Princess Bright Eyes." She caused a temporary rift in their relationship by refusing to allow distribution of the pamphlets.

Susette had strong feelings about another unrelated matter, and this resulted in a new set of contacts. She was much opposed to the use of alcohol, having seen the havoc it wrought in some Indian families. Because of her outspokenness on the subject of strong drink, she had become acquainted with Frances E. Willard, head of the Temperance Union in the United States. Now, in London, she was contacted by Lady Henry Somerset, who spearheaded the temperance movement in England. She wanted to schedule Susette for a series of temperance lectures in London. Susette at first refused, saying she lectured only on Indian subjects, but after being begged over and over, she finally consented to give one temperance lecture, but only one.

Lady Somerset engaged a large hall, and it was filled the night of Susette's appearance. She had her usual success and from it there later came a tremendously intriguing offer. After the London engagements had been fulfilled, the agent had a number of bookings available in other English cities, then suggested that they move on to Scotland.

They went first to Edinburgh, and their Presbyterian background soon gave them entry there. They were entertained as widely as they had been in London, often in the homes of nobility. Susette was still nervous about each new appearance, whether as lecturer or guest, but with her beauty and charm she had no difficulty in establishing rapport. She always carried an autograph book with her, and impressive names continued to fill the pages. Some people, noting her artistic interests, made little sketches as reminders of pleasant times they'd had with her. One note of sadness dampened Susette's enjoyment of the year abroad. Word reached them of the death of Nicomi. Now only Iron Eye and Mary remained in the home where she had once lived in a family of seven.

At the end of a year's time, Susette and T.H. returned to their home on Susette's allotment. It was a relief to her to get away from cities, back where she was close to nature. Some time before their trip abroad, T.H. had built her a proper house, a two-story frame. But she was to enjoy her house and the restfulness of the country for only a short time.

There was a scourge of grasshoppers that summer of 1888. To T.H. it was the last straw. He'd had enough of farming. He made a trip to Omaha and obtained a position on the newspaper he had left over ten years before to devote full time to the Indian cause. He found a renter for the farm, and he and Susette once again took up life in Omaha.

Chapter 20

RETURN TO THE CAPITAL

Susette was always loyal to her husband, of whom the members of her family were often critical. He disagreed with them on a number of issues, such as the Farleys' pasture project, a project in which Ed Farley successfully rented grazing land to people who needed pasture for their cattle. The result of these disagreements was that Susette's relations with her family often became strained. This was the situation at the time that the Tibbles moved back to Omaha. Susette missed the contacts with her family, particularly Rosalie. So it was to her joy that Iron Eye, not to be intimidated by family feuds, came to Omaha to visit her and T.H. and stayed with them for a number of days.

He brought news of Susan and Marguerite. The news of Susan was good. She wrote home often, telling not only about the courses she was taking, but also about the friends she was making both on campus and off, and about her social engagements. She loved her medical studies. She hoped the family could come back for commencement exercises when she graduated.

News of Marguerite was not so good. Her husband, Charles Picotte, was often ill, and his health did not improve over the years. There was fear riding with Marguerite much of the time as she taught her Indian pupils, fear that Charlie did not have long to live.

It was good for all of them, Iron Eye said, that Frank had his position with the Bureau of Indian Affairs. It provided them with a contact with the agency. And the work he was doing on the culture of the Omahas was gaining recognition; eventually Frank and Miss Fletcher expected to make a book of it.

Susette was very grateful for that time with her father. It was the last time she was to have with him. Although he was hale and hearty then, seeming in excellent health, a few weeks after his return to the reservation, he contracted pneumonia. After only a short illness, he died.

Not only was this a great personal loss to Susette, it also seemed to her to mark the end of an era. She felt a twinge of sadness for the loss of the Indian life she had known as a child. Yet that loss and the adoption of white people's ways was what Iron Eye had said must come and what his children had done much to bring about.

She thought her own contribution in bringing about the necessary changes in the Indians' situation was over. Her tribe, however, remained close to her heart, and she wished there was more she could do for them. Before long, this wish was to come true.

In the meantime, she followed her husband's career and helped him in whatever cause he was advocating, for T.H.

must be involved in a crusade. For a while it was a new political party, the Populists. This party supported the laboring class and farmers, and Tibbles, always for the underdog, took up the fight for them.

It was as a result of her husband's work with the Populist party that Susette again found herself in Washington. T.H. had been asked to report on Congressional hearings for a syndicate of weekly newspapers, and it was for this purpose that they went to Washington. It had been years since they had been active in the capital, and it was exciting to be back. While T.H. reported from the House of Representatives on Populist issues, Susette did the same from the Senate. This proved to be one of the happiest periods of her life. There was nothing in the work she was doing to frighten her. She had time to be with old friends and to enjoy concerts, art galleries, and the theater.

The years were ticking off. Susan, graduated from medical college, was back on the reservation, doing her best to meet the health needs of the Omahas. Rosalie, now with seven children, had no hesitancy in going to court when a legal problem arose in connection with the Farley pasture operation. She had sued more than one person who had cheated them. Marguerite was a young widow, continuing to teach.

Susette La Flesche Tibbles in her Lincoln, Nebraska, home

Chapter 21

OO-MAH-HA TA-WA-THA

Two unexpected, exciting challenges came to Susette in these latter days of her life. The first was the longed-for chance to do one more thing for the Omahas. It was important because it would commemorate the tribe. And it was an ideal project for her as it would employ both her writing and artistic abilities.

The city of Omaha was planning a summer's-long exposition to be called "The Trans-Mississippi and International Exposition of 1898," a world's fair on the grand scale of Chicago's, which had been held five years before. It would, among a multitude of other exhibits, treat the history of the city, beginning with its inception.

As the Omaha Indians were the first inhabitants of the area, and as the tribe's name became the city's name, they would receive recognition. As one means of doing this, Fannie Reed Giffin, an author and long-time friend of the Omahas, was planning to write a little book. She asked Susette to help her.

Together they laid out the plan of the book. They decided it should open with the all-important Treaty of 1854 between the Omaha Indians and the United States government. By this treaty, the Omahas voluntarily gave up the land on which they had been living just east of the Missouri River, and agreed to move to a location seventy miles north, which had been their reservation ever since. This move was negotiated because white people wished to develop a settlement on the banks of the Missouri.

This treaty had been signed (with their marks) by the leaders of the tribe, and Iron Eye was one of the signers. So the section of the book following the treaty, they decided, would be made up of brief biographical sketches of the signers. Here Susette's part in the writing of the book was invaluable, as it was in the next section, which was planned as a series of stories from the lives of the Omahas.

As the book grew, a pattern developed. There were many opportunities for illustrations, and Susette began sketching. Over twenty sketches of Indian life grew under her artistic fingers. First of all were the small ones at the opening of each chapter. These were tied to an over-sized capital letter, which was the first letter of the opening word. Susette particularly enjoyed the one she drew for the opening of her father's biographical sketch. It was of a little Indian boy leaning against a post. The "post" was the "I" of Iron Eye's name.

In addition to these little sketches, she did heads of the treaty signers and two full-length drawings, one of an attractive young Indian girl and one of a handsome Indian man. On both of these last she was careful to get every detail of the costumes accurate.

They called the book *Oo-Mah-Ha Ta-Wa-Tha*, Indian for

Omaha City. In the front of the book was an inscription that read: "Illustrations by Ishtatheanba (Bright Eyes) are believed to be the first artistic work by an American Indian ever published." Susette had won two firsts. She was the first American Indian lecturer and the first published American Indian artist.

Then something very different—the most challenging offer of her life—came to Susette. Frances Willard had not forgotten Susette's stand on temperance. She was offering her a world-speaking tour on the subject. Such an offer required very careful consideration and vital decision making. Names of countries that it would be wonderful to visit, such as Australia and New Zealand, were mentioned. What to do?

The temptation was tremendous. The trip would, for T.H. who was included in the offer as Susette's manager, be a dream come true. But Susette thought of the stage fright that she had never been able to conquer completely. And she seemed to be tired all the time. Did she have the strength for such an undertaking? There was also *Oo-Mah-Ha Ta-Wa-Tha*. Although her work on it was completed, she would like to be on hand when the book was launched.

Much as he yearned for Susette to say "Yes" to Frances Willard's proposition, T.H. did question whether or not she was physically able to undertake such a strenuous tour. Finally they came to their decision. They wrote Frances Willard that it was with deep regret that they had to say they would be unable to accept her wonderful offer.

101

A bust of Susette La Flesche Tibbles by sculptor Deborah
Wagner-Ashton (1984) is displayed in Nebraska Hall of Fame.

Chapter 22

HOME ON THE RESERVATION

The years were winding down and bringing their inevitable changes. Some of the changes they brought to the La Flesche sisters were sad, others happy. Saddest of all was Rosalie's death. She was so young, still in her thirties. But she had done more for her people than could have been expected in one twice her years. Both Marguerite's and Susan's stories of change were happy ones. Marguerite had remarried, taking Walter Diddock, the agency's industrial farmer, for her second husband. Susan had expanded her medical practice to include whites as well as Indians. She had married Henry Picotte, brother of Marguerite's first husband, and had two sons by him. She was dreaming of building a hospital; the need for one was great. Frank, with his job in the Office of Indian Affairs, provided a valuable liaison between Washington and his people. Perhaps even more valuable, however, was his work with Alice Fletcher as they continued their careful research of the Omahas' culture preparatory to the production of the classic book, *The Omaha Tribe*.

Susette longed for the country and T.H., seeing this, took her back to the reservation as often as possible. Still her spirits remained low. This T.H. could not understand. Her accomplishments were many and they should make her proud and happy. Much had been achieved for the Indians during the years of his and Susette's working for the cause:

Standing Bear's rescue from prison.

Defeat of the bill to remove the Omahas to the Indian Territory.

The Poncas' rightful lands restored.

The Severalty Bill passed.

Citizenship for the Omahas.

But Susette wanted citizenship for *all* Indians. That too would come, according to T.H., if not in their lifetime, later. And had they really done the right thing in following Iron Eye's directive to turn the Indians into whites? T.H. was sure they had, that this was the only way the Indians could survive in a world in which they were so vastly outnumbered by white people.

Unable to lighten Susette's depression by anything he said, T.H. finally suggested that they move back to the reservation. There was nothing that Susette would have liked better.

They moved in the spring, early enough so that Susette could watch the new leaves unfurl on the trees and violets dot the hillsides with purple. It was her favorite time of year, and it calmed her unrest and stilled her questioning.

Dr. Susan could see that her eldest sister was ill, but Susette insisted that she was only tired. With a feeling of enveloping peace, she watched the spring unfold. Thumbing through

Oo-Mah-Ha Ta-Wa-Tha and her thick autograph albums, she relived the years of her life, a life devoted to helping her people through a period of drastic change. It had taken courage and persistence, but it had been worth it. It was a good fight.

Susette La Flesche Tibbles, Bright Eyes, symbol of Indian liberty, died peacefully on May 26, 1903, at age forty-eight, in the house T.H. had built for her on her own plot of land.

Susette La Flesche 1854-1903

1854 Susette La Flesche is born on Omaha Reservation in Nebraska. By a treaty with U.S. government the Omaha Indians voluntarily give up their land and move to the Omaha Reservation some 70 miles north of the Missouri River. Kansas and Nebraska become U.S. territories. The Kansas-Nebraska Act limits area of the Indian Territory in present-day Oklahoma. Omaha is formally founded in the Nebraska Territory. Republican Party is formed at Ripon, Wisconsin. Crimean War begins (ended 1856).

1855 The first U.S. institution to grant academic degrees to women, the Elmira Female College, is founded at Elmira, New York. A campaign against the Sioux Indians is led by Colonel W. S. Harney. Henry Wadsworth Longfellow writes *The Song of Hiawatha*, based on the Finnish epic *Kalvala* and Iroquois traditions. Stanley Livingston discovers Victoria Falls in Africa. Ferdinand de Lesseps is granted concession by France to build the Suez Canal in Egypt.

1856 The Rogue River War forces most of the Indians in northern California and southern Oregon to accept living on reservations. Indian massacre of Potawatomie Creek, Kansas. The first railway bridge to span the Mississippi River is opened between Davenport, Iowa, and Rock Island, Illinois.

1857 James Buchanan is inaugurated as the fifteenth president of the U.S. The Indians stage a mutiny against British rule in India. Francis La Flesche, Susette's brother and famous American Indian ethnologist, is born near Bellevue, Nebraska (died 1932). Elisha Otis installs the first safety elevator.

1858 Minnesota becomes a U.S. state. An "Expedition Against Northern Indians" is carried out by U.S. army troops to discourage attacks on Washington state settlers. First Atlantic cable is completed by Cyrus W. Field, but it fails to operate. The Lincoln-Douglas debates are held in Illinois. The Suez Canal Company is formed. The National Association of Baseball Players is organized in America.

1859 Oregon becomes a U.S. state. First commercially productive oil well is drilled near Titusville, Pennsylvania. Charles Darwin writes *On the Origin of Species*. The steamroller is invented. Work on the Suez Canal is begun under the direction of Ferdinand de Lesseps.

1860 Abraham Lincoln is elected the president of the U.S. The first pony-express line is started between Sacramento, California, and St. Joseph, Missouri. The first horse-drawn tram begins operation. Skiing begins as a competitive sport.

1861 Kansas becomes a U.S. state. American Civil War begins (ended 1865). Seven Southern states set up the Confederate States of America with Jefferson Davis as president. Confederate forces repel Union forces at the Battle of Bull Run, Virginia. First transcontinental telegraph line is put in operation.

1862 The Santee Sioux in Minnesota rebel against mistreatment by white people on their reservation and kill about 800 settlers; as punishment, their land is confiscated and many Sioux are moved to Dakota Territory. Land Grant Act is approved, which eventually led to the establishment of the state university system. Swiss humanist Jean Henri Dunanat proposes the foundation of an international relief organization — the Red Cross. Many Civil War veterans settle in the Western states under free land terms of the 1862 Homestead Act.

1863 West Virginia becomes a U.S. state. Arizona and Idaho are organized as Indian Territories. Whitestone Indian battle in North Dakota. Civil War Battle of

Gettysburg, Pennsylvania. Lincoln issues the Emancipation Proclamation, freeing "all slaves in areas still in rebellion." Congress establishes free mail delivery. Roller skating is introduced to America.

1864 Nevada becomes a U.S. state. During the Sand Creek massacre of Cheyenne and Arapaho Indians in Colorado, some 900 cavalrymen kill 150 to 500 men, women, and children; the tribes were awaiting surrender terms when attacked by U.S. army. Union General William T. Sherman marches through Georgia. Abraham Lincoln is reelected president. "In God We Trust" first appears on U.S. coins.

1865 Confederate General Robert E. Lee surrenders at Appomattox, ending Civil War. President Lincoln is assassinated; he is succeeded by Andrew Johnson. The 13th Amendment, abolishing slavery, takes effect. Susan La Flesche, Susette's sister, is born (died 1915). The first railroad sleeping cars, designed by George Pullman, appear in the U.S.

1866 The 14th Amendment to the U.S. constitution prohibits voting discrimination, denies government office to certain Civil War rebels, and repudiates Confederate war debts. During Fetterman massacre a U.S. army detachment is ambushed and totally wiped out by the Indians in northern Wyoming. Ku Klux Klan is formed in Pulaski, Tennessee. Alfred Nobel of Sweden invents dynamite. Edgar Degas begins to paint ballet scenes.

1867 Nebraska becomes a U.S. state. Alaska is sold to the U.S. by Russia for $7.2 million. The British North America Act establishes the Dominion of Canada. Gold is discovered in Wyoming. Diamonds are discovered in South Africa. Livingston explores the Congo. The Paris World's Fair introduces Japanese art to the West.

1868 Washita Indian battle in western Oklahoma. Alabama, Arkansas, Florida, Louisiana, North Carolina, and South Carolina are readmitted to the Union after Civil War. The game of badminton is devised in England.

1869 General Ulysses S. Grant is inaugurated as U.S. president. Woman suffrage law passes in the Territory of Wyoming. First population census is taken in Argentina. Suez Canal is opened. Mahatma Gandhi, Indian nationalist leader, is born (died 1948).

1870 Women enter the University of Michigan, Ann Arbor, for the first time since its founding in 1817. Hunter College for Women is founded in New York City. Congress appropriates the first funds for federally administered education in Indian schools.

1871 Congress terminates the use of Indian treaties, and Indians are thereafter governed by congressional legislation and Executive Agreements. Great Fire destroys Chicago. Trade unions are legalized in Britain.

1872 The Modoc War (1872-73) between U.S. army and Modoc Indians, about their refusal to settle on Klamath Reservation in Oregon, ends with the hanging of tribal leaders. First U.S. national park — Yellowstone in Wyoming — is established.

1873 Major General George Crook successfully drives most Arizona Apache Indians onto reservations or into Mexico. First U.S. postal card is issued. First railroad reaches North Dakota, bringing many homesteaders.

1874 Gold is discovered on the Sioux Reservation; miners rush in. Adobe Walls Indian battle in northern Texas. The first American zoo is established in Philadelphia.

1875 England purchases Suez Canal shares. Rebellion begins in Cuba. A Civil Rights Act gives blacks equal rights in public places, though school integration is not included; Supreme Court declares the act invalid in 1883.

1876 Colorado becomes a U.S. state. Ponca Indians are moved from Dakota Territory to the Indian Territory in Oklahoma, where one-third of the tribe perish under harsh climate and scarcity of food. The Sioux Indian uprisings reach their peak when Chief Sitting Bull kills Custer's troops at Little Bighorn in Montana. Secretary of War William Belknap is impeached for taking bribes for the sale of trading posts in Indian Territory. The Indian Act is passed by the Dominion Parliament in Canada, recognizing the government's responsibility for health, education, and welfare of Indians. Alexander Graham Bell patents the telephone. Mark Twain publishes *The Adventures of Tom Sawyer.*

1877 Government gives Sioux Indians all Ponca lands in Dakota and Nebraska. Refusal of Oregon Nez Perce Indians to move to an Idaho Reservation leads to the Nez Perce War. Rutherford B. Hayes is declared the winner of 1876 presidential elections. Reconstruction of the South ends. After discovery of gold on their land, Sioux Indians are confined to several reservations, and the "Great Dakota Boom" begins (1879).

1878 As the result of the Bannock War, Bannock Indians are forced to return to their reservation in Idaho. Congress appropriates the first funds for Indian police forces. Thomas Edison invents the incandescent electric lamp.

1879 Ponca leader Chief Standing Bear and a group of his people return to Dakota without permission, where they are arrested and put into prison. In a landmark decision, *United States ex. rel. Standing Bear vs. Crook,* Ponca chief Standing Bear and his loyal friends are freed from prison. Susette writes her first newspaper article for *The World Herald* in Omaha; she accompanies her brother Francis and Chief Standing Bear on a tour of the East Coast cities on behalf of Ponca and Omaha; Susette successfully speaks against the forced removal of Indians to reservations and gives testimony to the Senate Committee in Washington, D.C. regarding forced removal of Poncas. With this lecture tour, she becomes the first American Indian lecturer. Susette writes her first story "Nedawi" for a children's magazine *St. Nicholas.* Amelia Tibbles (first wife of Mr. Thomas H. Tibbles) dies in Omaha, leaving two little girls. A large number of Indians are killed in an attempt by Chief Dull Knife (or Morning Star) and his band to escape an Oklahoma reservation and return to their northern homeland. Construction of the Panama Canal begins.

1880 Largely as the result of Susette's and Mr. Tibbles's efforts, a bill is passed in the Congress restoring land at Niobrora (Nebraska) to Poncas. Rosalie La Flesche, Susette's younger sister, marries Irishman Ed Farley. James Garfield is elected president. France annexes Tahiti.

1881 Susette delivers a paper before the Association for the Advancement of Women. President Garfield is assassinated; Vice-president Chester A. Arthur becomes president. Helen Hunt Jackson's *A Century of Dishonor* about mistreatment of Indians is published. Indian Shaker church is instituted in the state of Washington. Susette coauthors and edits *Ploughed Under: The Story of an Indian Chief* about Chief Standing Bear. Mr. Tibbles of *The Omaha Herald* and Susette are married on the Omaha Reservation in Nebraska. Francis La Flesche joins Bureau of Indian Affairs in Washington, D.C. Alice Fletcher arrives at the

Omaha Reservation for a detailed study of Omaha Indians. Sioux and Cheyenne resistance ends with the surrender of Sioux chief Sitting Bull, returning from exile in Canada.

1882 New York City installs first electric street lamps. U.S. bans Chinese immigration for the next ten years. A World Exhibition opens in Moscow, Russia. American Baseball Association is founded.

1883 World's first skyscraper, ten stories high, is built in Chicago and uses elevator invented by Otis. New York's Brooklyn Bridge is opened. The Orient Express, a train running between Paris and Istanbul, Turkey, makes its first run.

1884 France presents the Statue of Liberty to the U.S. Grover Cleveland is elected president.

1885 Almost unlimited power of the Indian police is curtailed by the Major Crimes Act of Congress. President and Civil War Union General Ulysses S. Grant dies. Louis Pasteur develops a rabies vaccine.

1886 Susette and her husband visit England and Scotland on a lecture tour and public appearances for American Indian causes. Susan La Flesche graduates from Hampton Institute and enters Women's Medical College in Philadelphia. Geronimo, an Apache Indian leader, finally surrenders—thus ending the long and bloody Apache wars of New Mexico and Arizona. Federation of Labor is founded. Canadian Pacific Railway is completed. Slavery is abolished in Cuba.

1887 The Dawes Severalty Act (General Allotment Act) is passed by the Congress (later amended in 1891, 1906, and 1910); the act jeopardizes the whole Indian reservation system; it grants citizenship to those Omahas who took land allotments. Area under tribal landholdings totals 138 million acres (reduced to 48 million acres by 1934). The first regulatory commission of the U.S., the Interstate Commerce Commission, is established.

1888 Susette and her husband move to Omaha where Mr. Tibbles once again starts a newspaper job. Joseph La Flesche, the Omaha chief (father of Susette), dies. Benjamin Harrison is elected president.

1889 South and North Dakota, Montana, and Washington become U.S. states. Oklahoma is opened to non-Indian settlement. Susan La Flesche graduates from Women's Medical College of Pennsylvania and becomes the first female Indian physician. Barnum and Bailey's circus opens in London, England. The first run for homesteading, by non-Indian settlers, takes place in Oklahoma.

1890 The last major conflict between Indians and U.S. troops, the Battle of Wounded Knee, takes place in South Dakota. For the first time U.S. census records the disappearance of a frontier. Daughters of the American Revolution (DAR) is founded in Washington, D.C. Japan holds its first general elections. Influenza epidemics flare up around the world.

1891 Earthquake in Japan kills 10,000 people. Famine sweeps Russia. Susan La Flesche starts working as a medical missionary to her tribe; she becomes a temperance speaker just like her sister Susette. Trans-Siberian railroad construction begins. In Java, Dutch anthropologist Eugene Dubois discovers *Pithecanthropus erectus* (Java Man), a variety of *Homo erectus*.

1892 Francis La Flesche graduates from the National University Law School, with a degree of law (Master of Law, 1893); he publishes the *Study of Omaha Music*. Grover Cleveland is elected president.

1893 The World's Columbian Exposition opens in Chicago. Henry Ford constructs his first automobile. Cherokee outlet run for homesteading by non-Indian settlers in Oklahoma. France acquires protectorate over Laos.

1894 Korea and Japan declare war on China. Hawaii becomes a republic, following a *coup d'etat*. Uganda becomes a British protectorate.

1895 Chinese are defeated in war with Japan. Cuba begins fighting Spain for independence. Mr. Tibbles establishes *The Independent* newspaper in Lincoln, Nebraska. King C. Gillette invents the safety razor. Armenians are massacred in Turkey.

1896 Utah becomes a U.S. state. William McKinley is elected president. Mary Church Terrell helps found the National Association of Colored Women. Klondike Gold Rush begins in Alaska. Susan La Flesche marries Henry Picotte, and moves to Bancroft, Nebraska, to practice medicine.

1897 William McKinley is inaugurated as U.S. president. First U.S. subway line opens in Boston. Severe famine hits India. Slavery is abolished in Zanzibar.

1898 Susette makes sketches and writes *Oo-Mah-Ha Ta-Wa-Tha* with Fannie Reed Giffin, thus becoming the first published American Indian artist. U.S. annexes independent republic of Hawaii. Spanish-American war begins, and ends in Treaty of Paris. U.S. acquires the Philippines, Puerto Rico, and Guam. Cuba gains independence from Spain.

1899 There are about 225 day schools and 148 boarding schools attended by 20,000 Indian children.

1900 William McKinley is reelected president. Bubonic plague epidemic breaks out in the U.S. Australian Commonwealth is proclaimed. Carry Nation, a Kansas anti-saloon agitator, begins raiding saloons with a hatchet. Francis La Flesche publishes his book *The Middle Five* (new edition, 1963).

1901 President William McKinley is assassinated; Theodore Roosevelt becomes president. First Nobel prizes are awarded from a fund given by Alfred Nobel, inventor of dynamite.

1902 Cuba becomes an independent republic. Aswan Dam opens in Egypt. U.S. acquires perpetual control over Panama Canal (which ends in 1999).

1903 Susette moves with her husband to her house on her own plot, on Omaha Reservation; she dies on May 26 in Lincoln, Nebraska, and is buried at Bancroft, Nebraska. Orville and Wilbur Wright fly the first airplane at Kitty Hawk, North Carolina. Settlement of Alaskan frontier begins.

INDEX-*Page numbers in boldface type indicate illustrations.*

Alcott, Louisa May, 46-47
Big Snake, death of, 39
Boston Indian Committee, 45, 54
Bright Eyes. *See* La Flesche, Susette
Bureau of Indian Affairs, 22, 70, 96
Chicago speaking tour, 27, 33-37
Clarkson, Bishop, 28, 40
Crook, General George, 78; meeting
    between Standing Bear and, 16-17
Dakota Territory, 10
Diddock, Marjorie, **61**
Diddock, Walter, 103
Dodge, Mary Mapes, 47
Dundy, Judge, "An Indian is a person,"
    ruling of, 29, 30, 56
Elizabeth Institute: education of Susette
    at, 15-16, 24, 56; graduation of Susan
    from, 77; Marguerite and Susan at,
    21-22, 49, 75; visit of Susette at, 49-50
Emerson, Ralph Waldo, 46
Farley, Ed, 50-51, 56, **60**; 68, 83-84, 95;
    interest of Rosalie in marrying, 16; **82**
Farley, Eddie, Jr., **60**
Farley, Jack, grandson of Iron Eye, **60**
Faneuil Hall, 48
Fletcher, Alice: **62**; appointment as
    special agent, 79; as author of *Omaha
    Tribe*, 103; and education for Susan
    and Marguerite, 79-81; friendship with
    Frank La Flesche, 67, 96; study tour
    of, on Omaha reservation, 71-74; and
    Susan's interest in medicine, 87
Fort Crook, 15
Fort Omaha, 15
Fraser, Reverend, 91-92
Fremont, Miss, **61**
Giffin, Fannie Reed, 99
Habeas corpus, writ of, 17, 19; hearing
    for, 20
Hale, Edward Everett, 76
Hamilton, William, 51, 56, 69
Hampton Institute, 73
Hemenway, Mrs., 54
Houghton (publisher), 46

Ikinicapi, Thomas, 84, 87
"An Indian is a person" ruling, 20, 30, 56
Indian rights, 17, 19-20, 43, 65-66, 67,
    79, 85
Indian Territory, 10
Iron Eye. *See* La Flesche, Joseph
Ishtatheanba. *See* La Flesche, Susette
Jackson, Helen Hunt, 46-47, 67, 78
La Flesche, Carey, **61**
La Flesche, Francis (brother): and
    forced move of Poncas, 10; as chaperon
    on first speaking tour, 22, 24, 34; **32**;
    58; **61**; **62**; friendship with Alice
    Fletcher, 67, 96; employment at Bureau
    of Indian Affairs, 70, 103; as co-author
    of *Omaha Tribe*, 103
La Flesche, Joseph (Iron Eye) (father):
    8; as chief of Omaha tribe, 9; and
    forced move of Ponca tribe, 9-11;
    offering of temporary home to Ponca
    tribe by, 13-14; decision to go to
    Omaha City, 15-17; and plight of Standing
    Bear, 19; at habeas corpus hearing,
    20; return to reservation, 21; and
    reaction to suggested speaking tour
    for Susette, 21-25; and importance of
    education to, 23-24; feelings of, toward
    whites, 41; need of, for new wooden
    leg, 50; expression of appreciation to
    Susette, 55; affection of Susette for,
    55-56; position of, on education of
    Marguerite and Susan, 79-80; and
    feelings of, on adjusting to white
    people's way of life, 85; visit of, with
    Susette and Tibbles in Omaha, 95;
    illness and death of, 96; as signer of
    Treaty of 1854, 99-100
La Flesche Picotte Diddock, Marguerite
    (sister): and forced move of Poncas,
    10; education of, at Elizabeth Institute,
    21-22, 42, 49, 75; desire of Susette to
    visit, 41; **59**; **60**; **61**; at Susette's
    wedding, 70; education of, at Hampton
    Institute, 79-81; interest of, in Charles

Picotte, 84, 87; engagement of, to
Charles Picotte, 87; marriage to
Charles Picotte, 88; and illness of
husband, Charles, 95-96; as teacher, 97;
remarriage of, to Walter Diddock, 103
La Flesche, Mary Gale (mother), 10, 23,
26, 27, 50, 51, 94
La Flesche Farley, Rosalie (sister): and
forced move of Poncas, 10; desire to
marry Ed Farley, 16; desire to stay on
reservation, 16; education of, 16;
letter of, to Susette, 41-42; wedding
plans of, 41-42, 50-51; wedding of,
54-57, 68; **58; 82;** life of, on reservation,
83-84, 88, 95, 97; children of, 83, 88, 97
La Flesche Picotte, Susan (sister): and
forced move of Poncas, 10; education
of, at Elizabeth Institute, 16, 21-22, 42,
49, 75; desire of Susette to visit, 41;
59; 60; interest of, in Hampton
Institute, 73; at Susette's wedding, 70;
graduation of, from Elizabeth Institute,
77; education of, at Hampton Institute,
79-81; interest of, in Thomas Ikinicapi,
84, 87; application of, to Women's
Medical College, 87; in medical school,
87, 95; graduation of, from medical
school, 97; marriage to Henry Picotte,
103; as Indian physician, 104-105; as
salutatorian of graduate class, 87
La Flesche, Susette (Bright Eyes): and
forced move of Ponca tribe, 9-11; as
interpreter for father, 15-16; education
of, 15-16, 23-24; at Elizabeth Institute,
16, 24; first meeting with Thomas
Henry Tibbles, 17; first attempt at
newspaper reporting, 19; at habeas
corpus hearing, 20; return to
reservation, 21; responsibility of, for
sisters, 21-22; as teacher, 24; on first
speaking tour, 21-25; at "Turning of
the Child" ceremony, 23; preparations
of, for speaking tour, 27; stage fright
of, 29, 35-36, 39; and telling of story of
Standing Bear on speaking tour, 28-31,
35-36; as interpreter for Standing Bear
in Chicago, 33-37; newspaper interview
of, 35-37; and reaction of audience, 31;
in Pittsburgh, 39-40; in Philadelphia,
40-43; homesickness of, for family and
reservation, 41; fondness for Thomas
Tibbles, 43, 45, 52; in Boston, 45-48;
writing of, for *St. Nicholas*, 49, 53; in
New York City, 49; visit with Marguerite
and Susan at Elizabeth Institute, 49-50;
work of, on *The Ponca Chiefs*, 51-52;
Tibbles desire to marry, 52, 53; need
for rest, 53-54; visit to reservation,
54-55; testimony of, before Congress,
53-54; attendance at Rosalie's wedding,
54-57; and second lecture tour, 65-66;
and passage of Ponca Bill, 65-67; meeting
with Helen Hunt Jackson, 67; friendship
with Alice Fletcher, 67; wedding plans
of, 67-69; wedding of, 69-70; and third
lecture tour, 71; and setting up of
study tour for Alice Fletcher, 71; visit
of Alice Fletcher with, 71-74; relationship
with Eda and May Tibbles, 75, 78;
autograph albums of, 78, 105; interest
of, in land allotment bill on fourth
lecture tour, 75-76, 78; writings of, on
Indian cause, 76, 78; illustrations of,
76; life in Omaha, 77-78; building of
house for, 80, 83; farming attempt by
husband, 84, 94; interest of, in European
tour, 84; and citizenship fight, 85; on
lecture tour in New York, 88; and
arranging of English-Scottish lecture
tour, 88-89; on English-Scottish tour,
91-94; and the temperance movement,
93; return to Omaha, 94; loyalty of
Susette to, 95; and death of father, 96;
involvement of, with Populists, 96-97;
involvement of, with "Trans-Mississippi
and International Exposition of 1898,"
99; and writing of *Oo-Mah-Ha
Ta-Wa-Tha*, 99-101; and decision not
to go to Australia-New Zealand, 101;
return to reservation, 103-104;
accomplishments of, 104; death and
burial of, 105
La Flesche, Susette (photographs): **2;**
with Frank, **32;** with Mr. Tibbles, **61;**
90; a bust of, in Nebraska Hall of
Fame, **102**

Longfellow, Henry Wadsworth, 46
Lowell, James Russell, 91
"Make-Believe White-Man Village,
  The," 9
Man Without a Country (Hale), 76
Martin, S.N.D., 69
Missouri River, 9
Nebraska, 9
"Nedawi," 49, 53
Nicomi, 10, 27, 50, 51; death of, 94
Niobrara River, 29, 51
Oklahoma, 10
Omaha City, 15
Omaha Indians, 9
Omaha Reservation, 13
Omaha speaking tour, 28-31
Omaha Tribe, 103
Oo-Mah-Ha Ta-Wa-Tha, 100-101, 105
Philadelphia speaking tour, 39, 40-43
Picotte, Caryl, **62**
Picotte, Charles F., **61**; 84, 87, 88; illness
  of, 95-96
Picotte, Henry, 103
Picotte, Pierre, **62**
Pittsburgh speaking tour, 39-40
Plains Indians, 48
Platte River, 10, 11
Ponca Chiefs, The, 51-52
Ponca Indians: forced move of, 9-11; life
  of, in Indian Territory, 13-14; return to
  Omaha Reservation, 13-14
Poppleton, J.M., 17, **18**, 19
Populist movement, 96-97
Ramona (Jackson), 67, 78
Read, Miss, 49
St. Nicholas magazine, 47, 49, 53
Somerset, Henry, 91
Somerset, Lady, 91
Standing Bear: **12**; and return of son's
  body for burial, 13-14; capture and
  imprisonment of, 15-17, 19-20; meeting
  with General Crook, 16-17; and habeas
  corpus hearing, 20; release from jail,
  21; on first speaking tour, 21-25; story
  of, on speaking tour, 28-31, 34; **38**; and
  death of brother, Big Snake, 39;
  decision to return home, 55, 65; visit
  of Susette and T.H. with, 73-74

Temperance movement, 93, 101
Temperance Union, 91
Tibbles, Amelia, 34; death of, 39-40
Tibbles, Eda, 34, 53; care of, by Bishop
  Clarkson, 40; and death of mother, 40;
  education of, 83; relationship with
  Susette, 75, 78
Tibbles, May, 34, 53; care of, by Bishop
  Clarkson, 40; and death of mother, 40;
  education of, 83; relationship with
  Susette, 75, 78
Tibbles, "T.H." Thomas Henry (husband):
  as assistant editor, *World Herald*,
  15-17; interest of, in Standing Bear,
  16-17; first meeting with Susette, 17;
  and reporting on plight of Standing
  Bear, 19-20; and habeas corpus hearing,
  19-20; arrangement of, with Iron Eye
  for speaking tour of Susette and
  Standing Bear, 22-25; plans for Omaha
  speaking appearance, 28-31; and
  description of Susette as Bright Eyes,
  33; and Chicago tour arrangements,
  33-37; and death of first wife, 39-40;
  and Pittsburgh tour arrangements,
  39; and Philadelphia tour arrangements,
  42; fondness of Susette for, 43, 45, 52;
  44; and Boston tour arrangements,
  45-48; as author of *The Ponca Chiefs*,
  51-52; Tibbles desire to marry, 52, 53;
  need for rest, 53-54; visit to reservation,
  54-55; testimony of, before Congress,
  53-54; **63**; and passage of Ponca Bill,
  65-67; meetings with others on Indian
  cause, 67; and decision of Susette to
  marry, 67-69; and third lecture tour,
  71; and setting up of study tour for
  Alice Fletcher, 71; visit of Alice
  Fletcher with, 71-74; and care of
  daughters, 75; fourth lecture tour of,
  75; writings of, on Indian cause, 76,
  78; return of, to Omaha, 77-78; and
  problem of education for daughters,
  83; building of house for Susette, 83;
  farming attempt by, 84, 94; interest of,
  in European tour, 84; and citizenship
  fight, 85; on lecture tour in New York,
  88; and arranging of English-Scottish

lecture tour, 88-89; on English-Scottish
tour, 91-94; return to Omaha, 94;
loyalty of Susette to, 95; involvement
of, with Populists, 96-97; and decision
not to go to Australia-New Zealand,
101; return to reservation, 104
Trans-Mississippi and International
Exposition (1898), 99
Turning of the Child Ceremony, 23
Wajapa, 73-74
Webster, John L., 17, **18**, 19, 68
White Swan, 10, 11
Whittier, John Greenleaf, 46
Willard, Frances E., 91, 101
Women's Medical College, 87
World Herald, 16

About the Author

Marion Marsh Brown grew up on a farm in Nebraska, loved her life there, and attributes much of her success as an author to those early years. Now a widow, she lives in Omaha. She has one son and three grandchildren.

For a number of years Mrs. Brown was a professor of English at the University-of-Nebraska-Omaha, but took early retirement in order to devote more time to writing. She continues, however, to lecture at schools and writers' conferences, and to conduct seminars on writing. She is a past president of the Nebraska Writers Guild and current historian of the Omaha Branch of the National League of American Pen Women. Mrs. Brown was recently chosen 1991 Woman of Distinction in Arts/Humanities by the Omaha Y.W.C.A. She has had a high school Pen and Scroll chapter named for her, and has had an A.A.U.W. Fellowship given in her name.

She is the author of eighteen published books, about two-thirds of them for young readers. Her books have won national awards from the National Press Women and National League of American Pen Women, and several have been chosen for publication by national book clubs.

Mrs. Brown's favorite leisure-time activities are reading, hiking, and traveling.